The Word in the Wilderness

The Word in the Wilderness

A Poem a Day for Lent and Easter

Malcolm Guite

CANTERBURY
PRESS
Norwich

First published in 2014 by the Canterbury Press Norwich
Editorial office
3rd Floor, Invicta House,
108–114 Golden Lane,
London EC1Y OTG

Canterbury Press is an imprint of Hymns Ancient & Modern Ltd
(a registered charity)
13A Hellesdon Park Road, Norwich,
Norfolk NR6 5DR, UK

www.canterburypress.co.uk

British Library Cataloguing in Publication data

A catalogue record for this book is available
from the British Library

978 1 84825 678 1

Typeset by Regent Typesetting
Printed and bound in Great Britain by
CPI Group (UK) Ltd, Croydon

Contents

Introduction   ix

Shriven, Ashed, and Ready for Action: Entering into Lent   1

Shrove Tuesday: Station Island XI *Seamus Heaney/
St John of the Cross*   3
Ash Wednesday: Ash Wednesday *Malcolm Guite*   7
Thursday: Stones into Bread *Malcolm Guite*   9
Friday: All the Kingdoms of the World *Malcolm Guite*   13
Saturday: On the Pinnacle *Malcolm Guite*   16

Week 1 A Pilgrimage Begins   19

Sunday: The Bright Field *R. S. Thomas*   21
Monday: The Pilgrimage *George Herbert*   24
Tuesday: Satire III *John Donne*   28
Wednesday: The Passionate Man's Pilgrimage
Walter Raleigh   31
Thursday: Maps *Holly Ordway*   36
Friday: The Song of the Wandering Aengus *W. B. Yeats*   40
Saturday: First Steps, Brancaster *Malcolm Guite*   44

Week 2 Deepening the Life of Prayer 47

Sunday: Postscript *Seamus Heaney* 49
Monday: Prayer *George Herbert* 52
Tuesday: Homecoming *Gwyneth Lewis* 55
Wednesday: Prayer/Walk *Malcolm Guite* 58
Thursday: How I talk to God *Kelly Belmonte* 61
Friday: The Pains of Sleep *S. T. Coleridge* 65
Saturday: Batter My Heart *John Donne* 70

Week 3 Dante and the Companioned Journey 75

Sunday: Late Ripeness *Czeslaw Milosz* 77
Monday: Meeting Virgil *Dante* 81
Tuesday: Through the Gate *Malcolm Guite* 85
Wednesday: Towards a Shining World *Dante* 88
Thursday: De Magistro *Malcolm Guite* 92
Friday: The Refining Fire *Dante* 95
Saturday: Dancing Through the Fire *Malcolm Guite* 99

Week 4 KnowThyself! A Conversation with Sir John Davies and Alfred Lord Tennyson 103

Mothering Sunday: Mothering Sunday *Malcolm Guite* 105
Monday: Why did my parents send me to the schools?
John Davies 108
Tuesday: What It Is To Be Human *John Davies* 112
Wednesday: The Light which makes the light which makes
the day *John Davies* 114
Thursday: Death as Birth *John Davies* 118
Friday: Faith in Honest Doubt *Alfred Tennyson* 121

Saturday: Strong Son of God, Immortal Love
    Alfred Tennyson   124

Week 5 Prayer that Pierces: The Point of the
         Passion   127

Passion Sunday: The Incarnate One *Edwin Muir*   129
Monday: Golgotha *John Heath-Stubbs*   133
Tuesday: The Agony *George Herbert*   136
Wednesday: Gethsemane *Rowan Williams*   139
Thursday: I wake and feel the fell of dark *G. M. Hopkins*   142
Friday: God's Grandeur *G. M. Hopkins*   145
Saturday: Love's as warm as tears *C. S. Lewis*   148

Week 6 Palm Sunday and Holy Week   151

Sunday: Palm Sunday *Malcolm Guite*   153
Monday: Jesus weeps *Malcolm Guite*   155
Tuesday: Cleansing the Temple *Malcolm Guite*   158
Wednesday: The Anointing at Bethany *Malcolm Guite*   161
Thursday: Maundy Thursday *Malcolm Guite*   163
Good Friday: XII Jesus dies on the cross *Malcolm Guite*   166
Holy Saturday: Two sonnets from the Stations of the Cross
    Malcolm Guite   168
Easter Sunday: Easter *George Herbert*   170

Appendix: Springs and Oases:
         The Saints' Days in Lent   175

27 February: George Herbert: George Herbert
    Malcolm Guite   177

1 March: St David: Miracle on St David's Day
  Gillian Clarke   179
17 March: St Patrick: St Patrick *Malcolm Guite*   182
20 March: St Cuthbert: Cuddy *Malcolm Guite*   184
25 March: The Annunciation: The Annunciation
  Edwin Muir   186

References   189
Acknowledgements   191

Introduction

Why might we want to take time in Lent to immerse ourselves in poetry, to ask for the poets as companions on our journey with the Word through the wilderness? Perhaps it is one of the poets themselves who can answer that question. In *The Redress of Poetry*, the collection of his lectures as Oxford Professor of Poetry, Seamus Heaney claims that poetry 'offers a clarification, a fleeting glimpse of a potential order of things "beyond confusion", a glimpse that has to be its own reward' (p. xv). However qualified by terms like 'fleeting', 'glimpse' and 'potential', this is still a claim that poetry, and more widely the poetic imagination, is truth-bearing; that it offers not just some inner subjective experience but, as Heaney claims, a redress; the redress of an imbalance in our vision of the world and ourselves. Heaney's claim in these lectures, and in his Nobel Prize acceptance speech, is that we can 'Credit Poetry', trust its tacit, intuitive and image-laden way of knowledge. I have examined these claims in detail elsewhere (*Faith, Hope and Poetry*) and tried to show, in more academic terms, how the poetic imagination does indeed redress an imbalance and is a necessary complement to more rationalistic and analytical ways of knowing. What I would like to do in this book is to put that insight into practice, and turn to poetry for a clarification of who we are, how we pray, how we journey through our lives with God and how he comes to journey with us.

Lent is a time set aside to reorient ourselves, to clarify our minds, to slow down, recover from distraction, to focus on the values of God's kingdom and on the value he has set on us and on our neighbours. There are a number of distinctive ways in which poetry can help us do that, and in particular the poetry I have chosen for this anthology.

Heaney spoke of poetry offering a glimpse and a clarification. Here is how an earlier poet, Coleridge, put it, when he was writing about what he and Wordsworth were hoping to offer through their poetry:

> awakening the mind's attention to the lethargy of custom, and directing it to the loveliness and the wonders of the world before us; an inexhaustible treasure, but for which, in consequence of the film of familiarity and selfish solicitude, we have eyes, yet see not, ears that hear not, and hearts that neither feel nor understand.
>
> (Coleridge, *Biographia Literaria*, Vol. II, pp. 6–7)

That wakening and renewing of vision is partly achieved by a change in the very way we read, which poetry asks of us. Poetry asks to be savoured, it requires us to slow down, it carries echoes, hints at music, summons energies that we will miss if we are simply scanning. In this way poetry brings us back to older ways of reading and understanding both the Word and the World, and to a way of reading, currently being revived in many churches, called *lectio divina*: a slow savouring of the text, a rich meditation on meaning that begins with the senses, with taste and sound. The great practitioners and preservers of this art, as of so many other vital arts, were the monks of Europe. They showed it visually in their illuminated manuscripts, and aurally in this practice of *lectio divina*, the prayerful form of reading aloud. The Benedictine historian Jean Leclercq describes it in this way:

> To meditate is to attach oneself closely to the sentence being recited and weigh all its words in order to sound the depths of their full meaning. It means assimilating the content of a text by means of a kind of mastication which releases its full flavour. It means, as St Augustine, St Gregory, John of Fecamp and others say in an untranslatable expression, to taste it with the *palatum cordis* or in *ore cordis*. All this activity is necessarily a prayer;

the *lectio divina* is a prayerful reading. Thus the Cistercian, Arnoul of Boheriss will give this advice:

When he reads, let him seek for savour, not science. The Holy Scripture is the well of Jacob from which the waters are drawn which will be poured out later in prayer. Thus there will be no need to go to the oratory to begin to pray; but in reading itself, means will be found for prayer and contemplation.
(The Love of Learning and the Desire for God, p. 90)

For the English Church, echoes of this ancient art of reading are preserved in the Prayer Book collect on the scriptures with its petition, 'Help us so to hear them, to read, mark, learn, and *inwardly digest* them' (The Book of Common Prayer Collect for the Second Sunday in Advent).

We should also come to poetry both for that inner nourishment and, in that beautiful Cistercian image, for waters drawn up from a well, to be poured out fruitfully later in our prayers.

As poetry begins to change the way we read, it also starts to influence the way we think and see. It becomes possible for us to enter into those moments of vision that are the beacons and turning points of our scripture, among which a moment of trans-figured vision in the desert – Moses turning aside to the burning bush – is the archetype of all transfigured vision. In a poem we shall encounter early in this Lenten journey, R. S. Thomas calls us to do just that:

Life is not hurrying
on to a receding future, nor hankering after
an imagined past. It is the turning
aside like Moses to the miracle
of the lit bush, to a brightness
that seemed as transitory as your youth
once, but is the eternity that awaits you
('The Bright Field')

I have several times used the metaphor of a journey, and particu-larly a journey through the wilderness. I would like to conclude this introduction by expanding a little on that and how the idea of journeying together through the wilderness has shaped the practice and meaning of Lent, and the form and content of this collection.

From the earliest times Christians have found in the story of the Exodus both an archetype of our redemption in Christ and a map of our inner life. That rousing call from Moses to his people to leave the slavery of Egypt, the Passover meal, the flight to the Red Sea, the going down into what they feared and emerging free, with their pursuers left behind them; and then the difficult but companioned journey through the wilderness towards the promised land, following the pillar of cloud by day and of fire by night; that whole sequence seemed to the early Church to show the pattern of Christian life. We are summoned by Christ to seek freedom from the slavery of sin, going down with him into the 'Red Sea' of baptism that drowns our sin but sets us free, and then learning intimacy and trust with our saviour as we journey with him through the wilderness that lies between our baptism and our final crossing of death's Jordan stream, and our entry into heaven. Christ's own 40 days in the wilderness seem to summon and take up the story. This whole understanding is beautifully distilled and expressed for many Christians in the hymn 'Guide me, O thou great Redeemer', with its evocation of the wilderness story: 'Let the fiery cloudy pillar lead me all my journey through'. The practice of keeping Lent for 40 days before Easter became a way of walking with Jesus in his wilderness journey – itself a participation, in solidarity with that first great exodus.

When God spoke to Moses from the 'lit bush' he promised, 'I will come down'; and come down he did, in Christ. Wherever we are in our wilderness journey, we are not alone; he walks with us, even as, in keeping Lent, Holy Week and Easter, we walk with him. What happened 'out there and back then' can happen 'in here and right now'. It may be that the poems in this book can be a little like the pillar of cloud by day, suggesting shapes, forming and reforming, but leading us forward. Or like the pillar of fire by night, a quickened wick, a kindling for good, a warmth in the cold and a light in dark places.

The shape of this anthology

This anthology, and so our journey, is divided into seven parts.

Shriven, Ashed, and Ready for Action

Before Lent proper begins, this first part takes us from Shrove Tuesday through Ash Wednesday and as far as the first Sunday in Lent. This is about clearing up and getting ready for the journey, confessing sins and being 'shriven', or absolved, which is what Shrove Tuesday was for. Turning around and facing the right way is what the 'repentance' of Ash Wednesday means, and what a reflection on Christ's own temptations in the wilderness helps us to do. Later in this anthology we will meet a variety of poets old and new, but for this initial section, reflecting before we start on the three temptations of Christ in the wilderness, I have used a sequence of three sonnets drawn from my collection *Sounding the Seasons*. Then comes the six-week pilgrimage itself. Each week the poetry develops or deepens the notion of our companioned journey.

Week 1: A Pilgrimage Begins

This first week introduces poems about pilgrimage itself and our life as pilgrimage. We reflect on maps and mapping, on how outer journeys and inner ones are linked, and what it is we learn from the landscapes through which we walk.

Week 2: Deepening the Life of Prayer

Herbert's wonderful and suggestive poem 'Prayer' begins a sequence of poems, some written in response to Herbert's own, that encourage us to reflect on and deepen our life of prayer: prayer as banquet, music, journey and conversation. The last sonnet in this section, John Donne's 'Batter My Heart', helps us think through those times when prayer seems to be nothing but struggle and conflict.

Week 3: Dante and the Companioned Journey

This week is given over to a conversation with Dante, the poet who so perfectly models our spiritual life as a companioned journey, in which we can be in present conversation with other writers and figures from the past. Indeed to quote from the introduction to that section: 'The whole of his poem the *Divine Comedy* is essentially an account of a companioned journey: one that begins in solitude, finds a friend, remembers a lost love and ends in divine Communion.' Using carefully chosen passages from Robin Kirkpatrick's lucid new translation, interspersed with some poetic responses to them of my own, we reflect on tenacity in our travelling, on the recovery of hope and the redemption of love. The context of the Dante passages is clearly explained, so there is no need to be familiar with his whole poem in order to appreciate this section; however, I hope readers may be inspired to pick up the threads of Dante's great poem and pursue it for themselves at their own pace afterwards.

Week 4: Know Thyself! A Conversation with Sir John Davies and Alfred Lord Tennyson

Then comes that time, which must be part of every pilgrimage or retreat if it is to be fruitful, when the old familiarities and comforts fall away, we leave behind the last desperate distraction, and finally face the big questions we so often evade. Who am I? What have I made, or am I to make, of my life? How might I face the valley of the shadow of death fairly and squarely yet still see and find a light to guide me through it? During this week we bring these questions to two poets who explored them deeply: Sir John Davies and Alfred Lord Tennyson. Both poets wrote longer poems that are full of wonderful and rewarding gems, which, because they are set in long poems, are very rarely anthologized. This week I bring some of these out, set them in context and share them more widely.

Week 5: Prayer that Pierces: The point of the Passion

Now, in Passiontide, Christ becomes all the more visibly our companion. We walk with him and see him face and overcome our own worst fears; we see him take on, in us and for us, the pain, the frailty, the fear, the failure, and the death itself that haunt and shadow our life. We stay with him through his Good Friday as he stays with us through ours, so that when Easter dawns we also share with him, and he bestows abundantly on us, the new life and light that death can never overcome and swallow; for indeed that new life has overcome and swallowed up death. In this section we pay particular attention to Gethsemane and the agony in the garden through a sequence of four linked poems. We start with Herbert's 'The Agony', move on to Rowan Williams' 'Gethsemane', which has the same setting and draws on Herbert's poem, followed by two of Hopkins' poems that also seem to be in close contact with the Williams poem. All four turn on the press and pressure of Gethsemane understood as an oil press, releasing God's mercy into the world.

Week 6: Palm Sunday and Holy Week

Properly speaking, Lent comes to an end on Palm Sunday, Holy Week being a season of its own, but since our poetic journey with the Word in the Wilderness has been so focused towards this end I include here a sequence of sonnets for every day of Holy Week, including Good Friday and Holy Saturday, drawn from my collection *Sounding the Seasons*. Then, on Easter Day itself, we return to George Herbert, a constant companion and guide, and learn with him that all our different days are somehow gathered into and redeemed in the one true day: Easter itself.

Sundays and Saints' Days

Every wilderness journey, though, and especially a long one like this, must have its springs and oases, its moments of refreshment, when we can turn aside from the toil and simply renew and delight in the vision that has drawn us here in the first place. This is what the Sundays and Saints' Days in Lent are for. Every Sunday is 'the first day of the week' – the day he is risen. Yes, we journey towards Good Friday, but we can do so fruitfully only in the light of Easter, for Christ himself went to the cross motivated by radiant love and 'for the joy that was set before him'. In this anthology I have made each of the Sundays the occasion for a visionary poem: a glimpse of heaven, a moment of transfiguration, something to renew our vision and keep us going. Likewise, however the date of Easter shifts, in any given Lent there are great feast days to keep and celebrate: the Annunciation, the feasts of David, Patrick and Cuthbert, the memory of George Herbert (and sometimes others, depending on how Easter falls). So I have provided an appendix called 'Springs and Oases: The Saints' Days in Lent', offering poems to be used in addition to or instead of that day's usual poem, on these special days.

Sources and Selection

The poems in this book are drawn from many sources; some will be familiar and others new. I have chosen some well-known 'classics' but also some poems from our past that in my view are especially pertinent now and have been unjustly neglected. Among these are extracts from Sir John Davies' great poem 'Nosce Te Ipsum' (Know Thyself) and from Tennyson's masterpiece of integration between doubt and faith, *In Memoriam*. There are poems by our contemporaries about the technology we live with, and poems by our distant forebears! Where the shape of our journey has called for a close or integrated series of poems, to reflect a clear biblical sequence, such as the three temptations of Christ in the wilderness, or the events in Holy Week, I have used poems from my book on the pilgrim year *Sounding the Seasons*, since they were written for that very purpose.

I hope that among these different voices some will speak personally to you, and that amid the music of the poetry you will find phrases that feed your soul, images that might become icons, windows into heaven to light your journey and welcome you home.

Shriven, Ashed, and Ready for Action: Entering into Lent

SHROVE TUESDAY

Station Island XI *Seamus Heaney/St John of the Cross*

As if the prisms of the kaleidoscope
I plunged once in a butt of muddied water
Surfaced like a marvellous lightship

And out of its silted crystals a monk's face
That had spoken years ago from behind a grille
Spoke again about the need and chance

To salvage everything, to re-envisage
The zenith and glimpsed jewels of any gift
Mistakenly abased ...

What came to nothing could always be replenished.

'Read poems as prayers,' he said, 'and for your penance
Translate me something by Juan de la Cruz.'

Returned from Spain to our chapped wilderness,
His consonants aspirate, his forehead shining,
He had made me feel there was nothing to confess.

Now his sandalled passage stirred me on to this:

How well I know that fountain, filling, running,
   Although it is the night.

That eternal fountain, hidden away
I know its haven and its secrecy
   Although it is the night

But not its source because it does not have one,
Which is all sources' source and origin?
   Although it is the night.

No other thing can be so beautiful.
Here the earth and heaven drink their fill
   Although it is the night.

So pellucid it never can be muddied,
And I know that all light radiates from it
   Although it is the night.

I know no sounding-line can find its bottom,
Nobody ford or plumb its deepest fathom
   Although it is the night.

And its current so in flood it overspills
To water hell and heaven and all peoples
   Although it is the night.

And the current that is generated there,
As far as it wills to, it can flow that far
   Although it is the night.

And from these two a third current proceeds
Which neither of these two, I know, precedes
   Although it is the night.

This eternal fountain hides and splashes
Within this living bread that is life to us
   Although it is the night.

Hear it calling out to every creature.
And they drink these waters, although it is dark here
  Because it is the night.

I am repining for this living fountain.
Within this bread of life I see it plain
  Although it is the night.

This is the day we think about being 'shriven' – confessing our sins and receiving the cleansing and release of forgiveness. The word 'shrove' drives from an Anglo-Saxon word, 'shrift', meaning to hear someone's confession, or 'shrive them'. So Coleridge's Ancient Mariner, when he makes it to land and needs to be released from the burden of his guilt, says to the hermit: 'O shrieve me, shrieve me, holy Man.'

It was the duty of priests especially to hear the confession and grant forgiveness and give spiritual counsel to those who were facing execution; when prison chaplains failed to do this properly, with time, care and attention, there was a complaint that people were being 'given short shrift', which is where that phrase comes from.

Here and now on this Shrove Tuesday we can take that time and care. But the whole idea of confession and absolution can seem strange and alien if it is not part of our life and culture, and sometimes daunting if it is! Sometimes it takes a poet to help us reimagine the possibilities of being 'shriven', really letting go, being truly forgiven. This poem is from Seamus Heaney's *Station Island*, a sequence of poems about confronting the past, letting it go in order to be released, freed and unburdened for the journey of life. The whole sequence is a masterpiece; but 'Station Island XI' is the jewel in its crown, containing as it does not only a fine emblem of sin and redemption but also a powerful new translation of perhaps the greatest of the poems of St John of the Cross.

The poem opens with the poet's memory of having ruined a kaleidoscope he had been given as a child, by plunging it 'in a butt of muddied water', in his desire, even then, to see into the dark. This gift, 'mistakenly abased', becomes an emblem for all that is ruined and 'run to waste' in us. The kaleidoscope becomes an emblem of the gift of imagination itself, an instrument in which we may see refracted through the creation the glories of God's light. Our fall, collectively and individually, has plunged this kaleidoscope into muddied water. The world we see habitually is not the true world at all, because it is seen through the sludge with which the kaleidoscope is encrusted, a sludge Coleridge so charitably called 'the film of familiarity and selfish solicitude'. The question is, has the gift been ruined for ever? Can the kaleidoscope surface again? Can it once more become the 'marvellous lightship', the window into heaven? That is a sharp question, both for each of us individually and for our whole culture. In this poem, Heaney suggests that it can: 'What came to nothing could always be replenished', and the replenishment, the restoration of vision, like the resurfacing of the kaleidoscope, is precisely the business of poetry.

The monk to whom Heaney has made confession understands this absolutely; he understands that Heaney's vocation as a poet comes from the same source as his own calling to be a monk, and is therefore able to say, 'Read poems as prayers'. It is not that Heaney is asked to, or would be prepared to, sloganize for the Catholic Church, but rather that this cleansing of the instruments of our vision by the power of his imagination as a poet is part of that whole restoration, even in our darkness, of the vision of Truth which is the work of the whole Trinity, and especially in us of the Logos, the Word who is also the Light. This becomes abundantly clear in the poem that Heaney goes on to translate, in which at last, after all his journeying, he arrives at and names the Source of that river that Milton named 'Siloam's brook' and Coleridge called 'Alph, the sacred river'. Perhaps we can see our own Lenten pilgrimage as a journey upstream to the source of that 'fountain, filling, running' that is celebrated in this poem.

ASH WEDNESDAY

Ash Wednesday *Malcolm Guite*

Receive this cross of ash upon your brow
Brought from the burning of Palm Sunday's cross;
The forests of the world are burning now
And you make late repentance for the loss.
But all the trees of God would clap their hands,
The very stones themselves would shout and sing,
If you could covenant to love these lands
And recognize in Christ their lord and king.
He sees the slow destruction of those trees,
He weeps to see the ancient places burn,
And still you make what purchases you please
And still to dust and ashes you return.
But Hope could rise from ashes even now
Beginning with this sign upon your brow.

It's a curious thing that we should use ash as a sign of repentance and renewal; surely it is nothing but the detritus of destruction! And yet it is so much more. The origins of the Ash Wednesday ash lie, of course, deep in the Bible, especially in all those Old Testament passages that speak of 'repenting in dust and ashes'. Sprinkling ashes on one's head was a sign of mourning and grief – the opposite of the oil of gladness – and went with 'rending' one's garments, a rejection of all those sleek tricks of self-presentation with which we seek to disguise our true selves from God and from others. And there is wisdom in that. I sometimes wonder whether instead of a brief ritual 'ashing' we shouldn't use Ash Wednesday as a day to rebel against our culture's obsessive concern with body image, presentation, clothing and appearance. Fashion models could be encouraged to dress as dowdily as possible, and we could all be invited to eschew the pressures of those 'photo-shopped' images of the impossibly thin and glamorous, resting instead on the inner beauty of simply being loved, at last, and in spite of all, by the maker of the cosmos. But there is deeper wisdom still in the tradition of ashing. For the ash that is left after purging fires is itself a fertilizer, a life-enabler, a source of new growth; we place these unpromising leavings on the garden and new things bloom. The cross of ash becomes a deeper symbol still, for what is destroyed in that emblem of all our destructiveness is sin itself. In a daring and beautiful creative reversal, God takes the worst we can do to him and turns it into the very best he can do for us.

In our own days of ecological crisis, the ash has perhaps acquired yet another layer of symbolic truth. As I set about the traditional task of burning the remnants of Palm Sunday's palm crosses in order to make the ash that will bless and sign our repentance on Ash Wednesday, I was suddenly struck by the way both the fire and the ash were signs not only of our personal mortality and our need for repentance and renewal but also of the wider destruction our sinfulness inflicts upon God's world and on our fellow creatures, on the whole web of life into which God has woven us and for which he also cares. Some of those themes are visited in today's sonnet.

THURSDAY

Stones into Bread *Malcolm Guite*

The Fountain thirsts, the Bread is hungry here,
The Light is dark, the Word without a voice.
When darkness speaks it seems so light and clear.
Now he must dare, with us, to make a choice.
In a distended belly's cruel curve
He feels the famine of the ones who lose,
He starves for those whom we have forced to starve,
He chooses now for those who cannot choose.
He is the staff and sustenance of life,
He lives for all from one sustaining Word,
His love still breaks and pierces like a knife
The stony ground of hearts that never shared.
God gives through him what Satan never could;
The broken bread that is our only food.

There are three days between Ash Wednesday and the first Sunday
in Lent, the first day of the first week of our six-week pilgrimage.
Since Christ's own primal Lent, his sojourn as the Word in the
Wilderness, is prefaced by his three temptations, by his confron-
tation with just those corruptions of the good that confront us
every day, it seems right to spend these three days reflecting on
these temptations, which will themselves form the readings and
subject for reflection in many churches this coming Sunday. I have
chosen to follow the order of the three temptations as they appear
in Luke's Gospel (Luke 4.1–12), which seems to me to make the
most spiritual and psychological sense. We start with the most

9

straightforward (and often most insistent!) of temptations: those generated by our bodily appetites and needs. We are tempted to serve first our own creature comforts, to tend to our obsessions and addictions before we have even considered the needs of others. Then we move on to the deeper temptations to serve and feed not just the body but its driving ego, with its lust for power, the need to dominate in the kingdoms of this world. We may have overcome the first temptation only because we are captivated and driven by the second. We diet, and discipline our flesh in gyms and health clubs, we submit our appetites to the dictates of personal trainers and three-month fitness plans, but only because we hope thereby to sharpen our image so as to shine and succeed in the world!

And then comes the last, the subtlest and worst temptation of all: that of spiritual pride. We may rise above worldly ambition only to congratulate ourselves on how spiritual we have become – how superior to our fat-cat neighbours! The very disciplines and virtues designed to bring us closer to our saviour, to make us more available as ambassadors of his love, become instead the proud possessions that separate us from the one whose strength is made perfect in weakness.

But this is to anticipate; let us go back to the beginning, with the temptation to turn stones into bread. Jesus meets this temptation with the profound reply, 'Man does not live by bread alone, but by every word that proceeds from the mouth of God.' This message certainly needs to be heard by Christians living in afflu-ent Western societies dominated by consumer culture. I believe that Jesus underwent this ordeal on our behalf in order to break open the ground of the heart and make real choice possible for us.

In this and the other sonnets on Christ's temptations I have borne in mind two essential but easily forgotten truths. The first is that because Jesus is both fully human and fully God there is a double aspect to each of these temptations. On the one hand Jesus experiences them exactly as we do, in a fully human way, feeling their full force and yet showing us both that it is possible not to give in to them and also the way to overcome them. As the letter to the Hebrews says: 'For we do not have a high priest who is unable to sympathize with our weaknesses, but we have one who in every respect has been tested as we are, yet without sin' (Hebrews 4.15). But at the same time he is God, and his action in defeating the devil in resisting the temptation, casting back the tempter, and creating and holding a space in which right action is possible, is done not just privately on his own behalf but with and for all of us. In the old Prayer Book litany there is a petition that says, 'By thy fasting and temptation, good Lord deliver us.' If Jesus were simply set before me as an example of heroic human achievement I would despair. His very success in resisting temptation would just make me feel worse about my failure. But he is not only my exemplar, he is my saviour; he is the one who takes my place and stands in for me, and in the mystery of redemption he acts for me and makes up, in his resistance to evil, what is lacking in mine. I emphasize this double aspect of the temptations in the beginning of this first sonnet, with a series of paradoxes that turn on the truth that it is God himself who feels and suffers these things for and with us:

> The Fountain thirsts, the Bread is hungry here,
> The Light is dark, the Word without a voice.

I have tried to bring out the way he endures these temptations both with us and for us. We 'must dare with him to make a choice', but at the same time 'he chooses for those who cannot choose'.

The second essential truth is that we should not see the temptations in entirely negative terms. The devil is no substantial being. A shadow himself, all he can do is cast shadows of God's substantial good. All good things come from God, and those things that the devil pretends to offer, but in the wrong way or for the wrong reasons, are cheap imitations of the very gifts that God does indeed offer and that Jesus himself receives, enjoys and, crucially, shares. He refuses to turn stones into bread for himself at the devil's behest, but later, in that same wilderness, he takes bread, gives thanks, breaks it, and feeds 5,000 with all they want, and 12 full baskets are left over! This was the substantial good from God, in light of which, and to gain which, it was necessary to refuse the shadowy substitute.

C. S. Lewis evokes this truth very well in *The Lion, the Witch and the Wardrobe*. Everything that the White Witch pretends she can give the children is a stolen and corrupted version of something that Aslan fully intends them to have in its true substance. She pretends that she will share the throne of Narnia with Edmund and then leave it to him, yet the whole story is about how Aslan will truly and substantially crown all four children kings and queens of Narnia. And this holds true in the smaller things too, even down to this matter of personal appetite. If Edmund had turned down the Witch's Turkish delight, he would have come sooner to Aslan's feast!

FRIDAY

All the Kingdoms of the World *Malcolm Guite*

So here's the deal and this is what you get:
The penthouse suite with world-commanding views,
The banker's bonus and the private jet,
Control and ownership of all the news,
An 'in' to that exclusive one per cent,
Who know the score, who really run the show,
With interest on every penny lent
And sweeteners for cronies in the know.
A straight arrangement between me and you,
No hell below or heaven high above,
You just admit it, and give me my due,
And wake up from this foolish dream of love ...
But Jesus laughed, 'You are not what you seem.
Love is the waking life, you are the dream.'

Then the devil led him up and showed him in an instant all the
kingdoms of the world. And the devil said to him, 'To you I will
give their glory and all this authority; for it has been given over
to me and I give it to anyone I please. If you, then, will worship
me, it will all be yours.' (Luke 4.5–7)

This second temptation is the lure of worldliness: 'success', money
and power set up obsessively on the throne of our hearts as rivals
to God. It is the supreme temptation of our own materially
obsessed culture. And it is our failure at this point that has led to

the gross imbalances between what has recently been termed the '1 per cent' and the '99 per cent'.

'To you I will give their glory and all this authority' is the dreadfully conditional offer that the devil still makes, and in my sonnet I try to flesh out in contemporary terms the types of figures who seem to be making and receiving that offer today, and the contexts in which this dreadful deal is transacted. It's striking to note that these old terms, 'worldly' and 'worldliness', are scarcely ever used in contemporary moral discourse. We still talk, and rightly so, about fairness, and fair distribution of resources. We are naturally concerned with justice and fair dealing in the worlds of finance, commerce and trade, but we seem to have lost sight of the long Christian tradition, and the substantial Christian teaching, that there is something essentially tainted and corrosive in the desire for worldly pre-eminence and success.

A symptom of this amnesia, this serious spiritual malaise that afflicts our culture, can be found in our extraordinary use of the word 'exclusive' as a positive term! The liberal West is allegedly the most inclusive culture that has ever existed: we deploy a great deal of rhetoric about including the marginalized, and take care that everyone should use politically correct and 'inclusive' language. But this is, of course, just a fig leaf. One look at the advertising in any magazine or on any website, one glimpse of the commercials that saturate our airwaves, tells a different story. Any estate agent advertising residential properties (or 'homes' as they like to call them – as though a home was something you could sell) reveals that their favourite word is 'exclusive'. Come and view these 'exclusive' flats. Or come with us on this luxurious and 'exclusive' holiday! And nobody asks, just who is being excluded? Nobody responds to these ads with a letter saying: 'I am interested in your product but perhaps I am one of those unfortunate people whom you and your exclusive clientele would like to exclude!' No one asks themselves, 'What is it in me that is being roused and appealed to here?' For it is not our generosity, our courtesy or our sense of community that is being worked on in this call to exclusivity. Rather it is the worst in us; our desire to be considered 'special' and 'better' and 'superior', at the expense of other people, is here being inflated and inflamed. In his chilling essay 'The Inner Ring', C. S. Lewis lays open this fallen desire in all of us to belong to exclusive clubs, cliques and circles, to be someone who is 'in', 'in the know', 'in the right circles', 'in on the real knowledge and power' among 'those who really count'; and to be able to look down on those who are 'out', excluded, not part of the magic circle. So much of the consumerism that chokes our society, bringing misery to the haves and the have-nots alike, is driven by this desire to have, to wear, to drive: to possess the status symbols, the 'exclusive' signs of belonging. Time and again goods and services are offered by manufacturers not for their intrinsic virtue, the beauty of their design, or the genuine pleasure that might be had from owning or using them, but for their 'exclusive' cachet, their 'exclusive designer label'.

Another word that is loved by worldliness and has in turn been subverted is 'dream'. We are to have 'dream homes', 'dream holidays', 'dream wedding days'. It is as if the purpose of dreams is to enmesh us deeper in the tangles of getting and spending, not to lift our vision, change our perspective and give us glimpses of heaven. I have tried to highlight some of these issues in this poem; here I see Jesus taking the worldly 'dream' on its own terms, calling us instead to wake up to the fullness of life. Perhaps only then can we, in Eliot's phrase, 'Redeem the unread vision of the higher dream.'

SATURDAY

On the Pinnacle *Malcolm Guite*

Temples and spires are good for looking down from;
You stand above the world on holy heights,
Here on the pinnacle, above the maelstrom,
Among the few, the true, unearthly lights.
Here you can breathe the thin air of perfection
And feel your kinship with the lonely star,
Above the shadow and the pale reflection,
Here you can know for certain who you are.
The world is stalled below, but you could move it
If they could know you as you are up here.
Of course they'll doubt, but here's your chance to prove it,
Angels will bear you up, so have no fear ...
I was not sent to look down from above.
It's fear that sets these tests and proofs, not Love.

The devil took him to Jerusalem and placed him on the pinnacle
of the temple, saying to him, 'If you are the Son of God, throw
yourself down from here, for it is written, "He will command
his angels concerning you to protect you", and "On their hands
they will bear you up, so that you will not dash your foot against
a stone."' Jesus answered him, 'It is said, "Do not put the Lord
your God to the test."' When the devil had finished every test,
he departed from him until an opportune time. (Luke 4.9–13)

If the first two temptations in the wilderness were in some sense
'obvious' – the temptation to mere physical satisfaction of

appetite, and to worldly success and power – then the third is subtle and dark, all the darker for pretending to a kind of light, or enlightenment. The third temptation takes place on the 'pinnacle of the temple', representing the height of religious experience and achievement. What could be wrong with that? But the best things, turned bad, are the worst things of all. A 'religious' or 'spiritual' life can be riddled with pride and a sense of distinction, judging or looking down on others, despising God's good creation! Such twisted religion does more damage in the world then any amount of simple indulgence or gratification by sensual people. One of G. K. Chesterton's wonderful Father Brown stories, 'The Hammer of God', explores this theme with his usual combination of acuity and humour. In the story a curate who has constantly taken to 'praying, not on the common church floor with his fellow men, but on the dizzying heights of its spires' is tempted to deal justice to his sinful brother by flinging a hammer down on him from those same heights. It is Father Brown who sees and understands the temptation and brings the curate down to earth, to a proper place of repentance. Here's a fragment of their dialogue before they descend:

'I think there is something rather dangerous about standing on these high places even to pray,' said Father Brown. 'Heights were made to be looked at, not to be looked from.'

'Do you mean that one may fall over?' asked Wilfred.

'I mean that one's soul may fall if one's body doesn't,' said the other priest ...

After a moment he resumed, looking tranquilly out over the plain with his pale grey eyes. 'I knew a man,' he said, 'who began by worshipping with others before the altar, but who grew fond of high and lonely places to pray from, corners or niches in the belfry or the spire. And once in one of those dizzy places, where the whole world seemed to turn under him like a wheel, his brain turned also, and he fancied he was God. So that, though he was a good man, he committed a great crime.'

Wilfred's face was turned away, but his bony hands turned blue and white as they tightened on the parapet of stone.

'He thought it was given to him to judge the world and strike down the sinner. He would never have had such a thought if he had been kneeling with other men upon a floor.'

'I mean that one's soul may fall if one's body doesn't,' said the other priest.

I was remembering something of this story when I wrote my sonnet on the third temptation, but thanks be to God that Jesus, in resisting this temptation to spiritual loftiness and display, shows his solidarity once and for all with all of us, trusting himself to our flesh and blood so that we can trust our flesh and blood to him. He does not look down on us, but looks up with the humble eyes of the child of Bethlehem.

WEEK I

A Pilgrimage Begins

pslams 120

FIRST SUNDAY IN LENT

The Bright Field R. S. Thomas

I have seen the sun break through
to illuminate a small field
for a while, and gone my way
and forgotten it. But that was the
pearl of great price, the one field that had
treasure in it. I realise now
that I must give all that I have
to possess it. Life is not hurrying

on to a receding future, nor hankering after
an imagined past. It is the turning
aside like Moses to the miracle
of the lit bush, to a brightness
that seemed as transitory as your youth
once, but is the eternity that awaits you.

Properly speaking, all Sundays are exceptions to Lent, for every
Sunday is a commemoration of the first day of the week, the
day of resurrection, and so really part of Easter. We should see
Sundays as little islands of vision in the midst of Lent, or per-
haps as little oases or pools of reflection and refreshment on our
Lenten journey; that is how I treat them in this anthology. So to
celebrate the first of them here is R. S. Thomas' famous poem
'The Bright Field'. This beautiful little poem brings us to the heart
of a gospel paradox and also takes us deep into the mystery of
time. The paradox is about losing to find, giving away to gain,

giving everything up only to find it given back in a new and more beautiful form. Jesus came again and again to this paradox in his teaching, and R. S. Thomas has responded in his poem to two parables told in quick succession in Matthew's Gospel:

> The kingdom of heaven is like treasure hidden in a field, which someone found and hid; then in his joy he goes and sells all he has and buys that field. Again, the kingdom of heaven is like a merchant in search of fine pearls; on finding one pearl of great value, he went and sold all that he had and bought it. (Matthew 13.44–46)

The beauty of these parables is that they fill out the positive form that redeems what might seem to be the pure negativity of 'giving up' and 'selling all' which informs our Lenten abstinence. The gospel is not about giving up and going without for its own sake; it is about making room for something wonderful. It is about clearing out the clutter, not only making the space but taking the time for the kingdom that might seem tiny as a mustard seed but will prove, in due course, to be the great branching tree in whose canopy we all find a place. But we must glimpse the seed, buy the field, take the time, and not lose it all by 'hurrying by'.

It is fascinating to see what Thomas has done with these parables, how their familiar terms are refracted in his poetic imagination, and re-presented, glowing anew and fused now with that other archetypal moment and glimpse of heaven, the story of Moses and the burning bush.

He wins us, to begin with, by confession of what we have all done. These are not the proud words of some exclusive mystic who has 'got' the vision when others haven't; rather he confesses that he too has 'seen the sun break through' but also, like us, 'gone my way and forgotten it'. But, paradoxically, he has not really forgotten it. The very writing and sharing of the poem shows that, and if he too, even in the making of this poem, can find it again then so can we in reading it. As the poem moves from the past to the present tense, from 'I have seen ...' to 'I realise now ...', we are called, even as we read it, into the present continuous, to that 'turning aside like Moses to the miracle of the lit bush'. Elizabeth Barrett Browning in her long poem *Aurora Leigh* also brings us to such a moment; indeed, she takes it further, suggesting that these glimpses of glory are not just a wistful one-off in an otherwise empty desert but are richly available to us always and everywhere, if only we have eyes to see and time to stop:

> Earth's crammed with heaven,
> And every common bush afire with God;
> But only he who sees, takes off his shoes,
> (*Aurora Leigh*, lines 61–3)

Thomas concludes his little free verse sonnet (even its form is a paradox!) with a further paradox about time that is perhaps the most beautiful and hopeful thing in the poem. He points to

> a brightness
> that seemed as transitory as your youth
> once, but is the eternity that awaits you.

Here we discover that what we thought was lost and receding is in reality still ahead of us; we are not declining towards a sunset, but travelling towards the dawn!

MONDAY

The Pilgrimage *George Herbert*

I travell'd on, seeing the hill, where lay
    My expectation.
  A long it was and weary way.
  The gloomy cave of Desperation
I left on th'one, and on the other side
    The rock of Pride.

And so I came to Fancy's meadow strow'd
    With many a flower:
  Fair would I here have made abode,
  But I was quicken'd by my houre.
So to Care's copse I came, and there got through
    With much ado.

That led me to the wild of Passion, which
    Some call the wold; *wild*
  A wasted place, but sometimes rich.
  Here I was robb'd of all my gold,
Save one good Angel, which a friend had ti'd
    Close to my side.

At length I got unto the gladsome hill,
    Where lay my hope,
  Where lay my heart; and climbing still,
  When I had gain'd the brow and top,
A lake of brackish waters on the ground
    Was all I found.

With that abash'd and struck with many a sting
  Of swarming fears,
I fell, and cry'd, Alas my King;
Can both the way and end be tears?
Yet taking heart I rose, and then perceiv'd
  I was deceiv'd:

My hill was further: so I flung away,
  Yet heard a crie
Just as I went, *None goes that way*
And lives: If that be all, said I,
After so foul a journey death is fair,
  And but a chair.

We are considering Lent as a journey, or a pilgrimage, like Israel's
or Christ's journey through the wilderness. Poetry can help us be
honest about how round-about and sometimes tiring that journey
is, and how the goal itself seems to shift. I love this poem by
George Herbert; it makes me feel that when I'm tired and dis-
oriented he has been in that place too, so at least I am in good
company!

Although he often uses emblems and little allegorical vignettes,
it is rare that Herbert writes such direct and sustained allegory,
and some scholars believe that this sustained account of life as
a pilgrim journey, passing between 'the gloomy cave of Desper-
ation' and 'the rock of Pride', dallying in 'Fancy's meadow' and
getting through 'Care's copse', may well have been the inspiration
for John Bunyan's more famous *Pilgrim's Progress*. Here we have
that book in advance and in miniature, as it were, but it may be
that Herbert's mapping exercise will help us to orient ourselves,
and guide us a little on the way.

The poem starts without preamble, *in medias res*, right in the
midst of the journey (like Dante), with the words 'I travell'd on';
Herbert, like us, has already been some distance on a long and
weary way. There is real psychological and spiritual insight in his
pairing of the 'rock of Pride' and the 'cave of Desperation'. Both
pride and despair are forms of self-absorption and the Christian

must try to steer between them, hard though it is. The second verse again shows his clarity and common touch. Like most of us he would like to stay and stray, and make his abode in 'Fancy's meadow', those places in life that seem rich with leisure and variety; like most of us he finds that he is 'quicken'd by my houre'. Time hurries on, the next appointment calls, things have to be done, and more often than not even a brief dalliance in 'Fancy's meadow' is followed by a hard slog through 'Care's copse'; the anxieties and difficulties of our life are likened to a close-grown and entangling thicket of woodland. No sooner have we 'got through' that with 'much ado' then there is another potential danger and diversion on our way.

In the third verse, in describing 'the wild of Passion' Herbert avails himself of a series of wordplays that may not be clear to us in modern English. In Herbert's day spelling was not fixed, and 'wild' and 'willed', 'wold' and 'would' could all be spelled the same way! So Passion is described as a 'wild' place or a wilderness, but the word 'wild' then modulates to 'wold', an elevated tract of open country, but punning on 'would'. The passions drive us to do what we 'would', just as for Herbert 'wild' also puns on 'willed'. The 'wild wold' is described as both 'a wasted place' and yet also 'sometimes rich'. This ambiguity is absolutely true to its subject. We all know about the waste and devastation, in broken marriages and broken lives, that result from uncontrolled passion, but also recognize our states of heightened emotion as being 'sometimes rich'. Running deep under all these careful ambiguities is that of the word 'Passion' itself, which means both powerful human feeling and, in the older sense, 'suffering': what happens or is done unto us, and supremely the Passion of Christ. Perhaps Herbert is showing that while there is much to be lost, there is also much to be learned – even a kinship with Christ in all our Passion. Certainly he seems to hint at this in the final pun or wordplay of this verse, which turns on 'Angel'. The Angel was the name of a gold coin in Herbert's day, which bore the image of an angel.

Here I was robb'd of all my gold,
Save one good Angel, which a friend had ti'd
Close to my side.

Herbert seems to be pointing both to the truth that we may be ruined or impoverished by uncontrolled passion (or addiction!), and to the fact that somehow through it all we may be companioned by Christ, the true Friend, tied to us as the guardian angel of his accompanying love from which we will not be parted. For all its antiquated English, this verse speaks directly into modern life.

The following verses take us deeper and deal with one of the constant experiences of our life: disappointment. When, after all this trouble and coming through all these dangers he finally surmounts 'the gladsome hill, where lay my hope' he finds nothing but 'a lake of brackish waters on the ground' – no more than the saltiness of his own tears and sweat. He's ready to give up, but still, even in this disappointment, he cries to God: 'Alas my King'. He gives voice to his complaint, something we don't always do. And then, out of this very disappointment, and from its new perspective, comes a renewal of vision, the pilgrim takes heart, and sees that there are greater heights, and the true hill is further off.

Then comes the final twist in the plot, and turn of the poem, seemingly bleak but full of hidden grace. As the pilgrim sets off afresh he is reminded of his mortality by a seemingly forbidding voice that cries, 'None goes that way and lives', but the pilgrim turns the warning around in two senses. The first, seemingly downbeat, in which he calls death 'a chair', might seem to be saying no more than 'well, at least I'll have a break from all this hard slog'. But in the seventeenth century 'a chair' could also mean something more than that: a litter, or even a carriage, a means whereby we not only rest but are carried forward. Indeed, some commentators think that Herbert may have been thinking of the chariot of fire in 2 Kings 2.11, that will lift the pilgrim, like Elijah, beyond the low hills of his expectation into the true mountain country of heaven.

TUESDAY

Satire III *John Donne*

... though truth and falsehood be
Near twins, yet truth a little elder is;
Be busy to seek her; believe me this,
He's not of none, nor worst, that seeks the best.
To adore, or scorn an image, or protest,
May all be bad; doubt wisely; in strange way
To stand inquiring right, is not to stray;
To sleep, or run wrong, is. On a huge hill,
Cragged and steep, Truth stands, and he that will
Reach her, about must and about must go,
And what the hill's suddenness resists, win so.
Yet strive so that before age, death's twilight,
Thy soul rest, for none can work in that night.
To will implies delay, therefore now do;
Hard deeds, the body's pains; hard knowledge too
The mind's endeavours reach, and mysteries
Are like the sun, dazzling, yet plain to all eyes.

Monday's poem, 'The Pilgrimage' by George Herbert, introduced
a Lenten theme of journey and search, reflecting the journey of
the children of Israel through the wilderness, and Jesus' own 40
days in the wilderness. Our poems this week develop that theme
further, beginning with this extract from one of John Donne's
Satires. This poem uses the same image of truth on a hill; indeed
it may be one of the sources for Herbert, who knew Donne well
as a family friend. The wider context of this 'Satire' is Donne's

difficult and perplexed search, amid the many controversies that vexed the Church in his day, for a clear understanding of where Christ is to be found. Here he realizes that a round-about method, considering the same thing from different places and angles, may be the only way to ascend to truth, but he also recognizes the need for resolve, deliberation and energy in the search. This is a dense and complex poem; I have chosen this particular passage because of its two clear, striking and helpful metaphors of the hill and the sun.

But first let me explain a little context. Earlier in the 'Satire' Donne conjures up caricatures of various contemporary religious 'types': an extreme Roman Catholic besotted with ritual and all things Roman, an extreme Calvinist who believes nothing unless it's come straight from Geneva, and a lazy indifferentist who blithely assumes that all faiths probably add up to the same thing but doesn't actually bother to enquire. In the course of the poem Donne shows how each of them might be mistaken or simply carried away. Then, seeing this variety, Donne confronts the possibility of never finding any truth or certainty. Finally, we come to the point in the poem where our extract begins, in which he realizes that however difficult, or tentative, he must begin to make serious enquiries. Truth and falsehood may be, as he says, 'near twins', so like each other that it's hard to distinguish, but truth is 'a little elder' and she's still worth seeking.

That truth 'a little elder is', is itself a statement that carries a great truth. Truth can exist without falsehood, but to discern anything as actually false we have to have a prior standard of truth; every falsehood points to, and depends upon, an 'elder' truth. Donne tells himself that he must be 'busy to seek' truth. Earlier in the 'Satire' he may have mocked those who 'adore, or scorn an image, or protest', but that does not absolve him of responsibility to seek truth for himself. Then comes one of the great phrases of this poem: 'doubt wisely; in strange way to stand inquiring right, is not to stray'. The Church would do well to learn from this. The serious doubter, the sincere enquirer, the person who hesitates a long time on a threshold, these are all people to be honoured and encouraged, not, as is so often the case, either demonized or cajoled. Donne put this even more succinctly in one of his great sermons at Lincoln's Inn: 'To come to a doubt and a debatement in any religious duty is the voice of God in our conscience. Would you know the truth? Doubt and then you will enquire ...' (Sermons 5.38).

Then comes the justly famous metaphor of the hill:

On a huge hill,
Cragged and steep, Truth stands, and he that will
Reach her, about must and about must go,
And what the hill's suddenness resists, win so.

Some things are too great to come at directly. Just as we may weave back and forth as we climb a hill, and appear to be going round in circles, yet all the while are coming closer to the summit, so in our religious and spiritual life things may seem circuitous; we may think we have come back to the same spot, but always, if we press on, it is a little higher, a little closer to the truth.

Donne follows this image with a reflection on light. Perhaps the metaphor of an arduous climb suggested the desire to reach the peak before twilight; then comes the direct allusion to John 9.4: 'We must work the works of him who sent me while it is day; night comes when no one can work.'

And that leads on to the beautiful image of the sun, 'dazzling, yet plain to all eyes'. C. S. Lewis would have been very familiar with this poem, and I wonder if these lines of Donne's are the distant ancestor of one of his famous and illuminating sayings: 'I believe in Christianity as I believe that the sun has risen, not only because I see it but because by it I see everything else' ('Is Theology Poetry').

WEDNESDAY

The Passionate Man's Pilgrimage *Walter Raleigh*

Give me my scallop shell of quiet,
  My staff of faith to walk upon,
My scrip of joy, immortal diet,
  My bottle of salvation,
My gown of glory, hope's true gage;
And thus I'll take my pilgrimage.

Blood must be my body's balmer,
  No other balm will there be given;
Whilst my soul, like a quiet palmer,
  Travelleth towards the land of heaven;
Over the silver mountains,
Where spring the nectar fountains:
    There will I kiss
    The bowl of bliss;
And drink mine everlasting fill
Upon every milken hill:
My soul will be a-dry before;
But after, it will thirst no more.
Then by that happy blestful day,
  More peaceful pilgrims I shall see,
That have cast off their rags of clay,
  And walk apparelled fresh like me.
    I'll take them first
    To quench their thirst,
And taste of nectar suckets,

> At those clear wells
> Where sweetness dwells
Drawn up by saints in crystal buckets.

And when our bottles and all we
Are filled with immortality,
Then the blessed paths we'll travel,
Strowed with rubies thick as gravel;
Ceilings of diamonds, sapphire floors,
High walls of coral, and pearly bowers.
From thence to heavens's bribeless hall,
Where no corrupted voices brawl;
No conscience molten into gold,
No forged accuser bought or sold,
No cause deferred, nor vain-spent journey;
For there Christ is the King's Attorney,
Who pleads for all without degrees,
And he hath angels, but no fees.
And when the grand twelve-million jury
Of our sins, with direful fury,
'Gainst our souls black verdicts give,
Christ pleads his death, and then we live.

Be thou my speaker, taintless pleader,
Unblotted lawyer, true proceeder!
Thou giv'st salvation even for alms;
Not with a bribèd lawyer's palms.
And this is my eternal plea
To him that made heaven, earth, and sea,
That, since my flesh must die so soon,
And want a head to dine next noon,
Just at the stroke, when my veins start and spread,
Set on my soul an everlasting head.
Then am I ready, like a palmer fit;
To tread those blest paths which before I writ.

We continue with our theme of pilgrimage, and follow the hint given by George Herbert that the last stage of our pilgrimage will be the leaving of this life to arrive at our true end and best beginning in heaven. 'The Passionate Man's Pilgrimage' is one of a group of poems believed to have been written by Sir Walter Raleigh (1554–1618) while imprisoned in the Tower.

Though formal, outward and visible pilgrimage had been forbidden in England after the Reformation, it would seem that Raleigh, possibly writing on the eve of his execution, dared to revive all its traditional catholic imagery, but applied it instead to the inward and spiritual pilgrimage, and particularly the journey to heaven through the grave and gate of death, a journey he was preparing to make. He believed himself to be the victim of a miscarriage of justice, and the beautiful turn at the end of this poem in which Christ becomes 'the King's Attorney' to plead for all is particularly poignant.

Raleigh begins his poem with a litany of the traditional garb and symbols of the pilgrim, each of which is quietly transfigured into an essential aspect of Christian life and faith, open to all whether they are outwardly pilgrims or not. The scallop shell is the symbol of St Iago de Compostella, whose shrine was (and remains) one of the great pilgrimage sites; it is so well known that the road to it is simply known as the Camino, the Way. So the scallop shell became the symbol of all pilgrimage, and even now in many churches both Catholic and Anglican a scallop shell is dipped into the font at baptism to signify the beginning of a pilgrim life. The calming and beautiful repetition of the word 'quiet' in the opening verses is particularly poignant if, as internal evidence suggests (lines 53–4), Raleigh was indeed composing this poem just before his death. One can imagine the mood swings, the dread, the panic, the heart beating, the blood racing, which he would be struggling to overcome and transform in the composition of this quiet poem. And indeed he does so not by evading but by facing the vivid images of blood and beheading that must have been racing through his mind; like most Elizabethans he would have witnessed such executions. So he writes, 'Blood must be my body's balmer', and even more vividly, 'Just at the stroke, when my veins start and spread, set on my soul an everlasting head'. But for all these vivid and visceral moments, the overall tone of the poem is serene and beautiful. Even the implicit denunciation of the court is ultimately focused on Christ who, unlike the officials of the kangaroo court in which he was tried, would be a 'taintless pleader'. For modern readers the 'sapphire floors' and 'pearly bowers' may seem a little cloying, though all these images are drawn from and reflect scripture.

I am moved by the image of 'those clear wells, where sweetness dwells', recalling as it does the promise in Isaiah 12.3, 'with joy you will draw water from the wells of salvation'; and the description of the peaceful pilgrims, newly apparelled, drawing closer to one another, delighted and refreshed, on the final stage of their journey into heaven. Then comes the reflection, looking back and looking forward, when Raleigh speaks of

From thence to heavens's bribeless hall,
Where no corrupted voices brawl;
No conscience molten into gold,
No forged accuser bought or sold,

Raleigh had been accused, by the confession of a friend, of involvement in a plot against King James, though the evidence was hearsay. He defended himself but was never allowed to face or cross-examine his accuser. But even at the moment when he is recognizing earthly fraud and corruption he sees that the very light of heaven that enables him to see it promises something better. Pursuing the theme of heaven as the true court, he gives us one of the most beautiful and scripturally based accounts of Christ as our redeemer, both pleading for us against the jury of our sins, and offering himself, in our stead:

For there Christ is the King's Attorney,
Who pleads for all without degrees,
And he hath angels, but no fees.
And when the grand twelve-million jury
Of our sins, with direful fury,

'Gainst our souls black verdicts give,
Christ pleads his death, and then we live.

There could not be a clearer account of our salvation than this,
offered on the eve of his death, by a man who was accused by
many of his contemporaries of atheism!

THURSDAY

Maps *Holly Ordway*

Antique maps, with curlicues of ink
As borders, framing what we know, like pages
From a book of travelers' tales: look,
Here in the margin, tiny ships at sail.
No-nonsense maps from family trips: each state
Traced out in color-coded numbered highways,
A web of roads with labeled city-dots
Punctuating the route and its slow stories.
Now GPS puts me right at the centre,
A Ptolemaic shift in my perspective.
Pinned where I am, right now, somewhere, I turn
And turn to orient myself. I have
Directions calculated, maps at hand:
Hopelessly lost till I look up at last.

Holly Ordway's contemporary sonnet brings us back from the
seventeenth century to our own fast-moving, wi-fi, online times,
and calls us sharply to look up from our screens and be more truly
oriented. Ordway, an American poet and academic, surprised her
colleagues in secular academia by becoming a Christian, a story
she tells in her book *Not God's Type: An Atheist Academic Lays
Down Her Arms*. She now teaches 'Imaginative Apologetics',
which is concerned with the way in which the experience of the
imaginative arts both makes the case and prepares the heart for a
return to faith in God.

This beautiful blank sonnet takes us on a journey through history, embodied in three maps, and then brings us abruptly to ourselves in the present, with an implicit word of challenge. We begin with the antique maps, with their 'curlicues of ink', and little drawings of ships, evocative of a bygone era, a different view of the world, perhaps going back to a time when the earth was thought to be the centre of all things, or even to be flat, with the seas pouring off its edges. Then she brings us into the twentieth century with the road maps that most of us can remember, 'no-nonsense maps from family trips', quietly evoking the sense of shared conversation and storytelling in the family car and the way the map itself is like a keeper or an index of memories: 'with labeled city-dots punctuating the route and its slow stories'.

Then comes the 'volta', or the 'turn'. There is a strong tradition in the making of sonnets to see the transition from the first eight lines (the octet) to the final six (the sextet) as a point of transition, offering a turn in the meaning, tone or development of the poem. The early Italian pioneers of the sonnet form called this the 'volta', and some of the most famous sonnet rhyme schemes, such as the Petrarchan form, are designed to emphasize this moment of turning, which is often indicated by a shift in the writer's perspective. So at her 'volta', Ordway shifts from the past to the present tense, announced with opening word 'Now', and in every sense introduces a profound shift of perspective. Suddenly we have come out of the world of maps and into the twenty-first-century world of satnav! Even though many centuries may have separated the 'antique maps, with curlicues of ink' from the 'no-nonsense' road maps, they still have more in common with each other and belong, as it were, to the same era, in comparison with the new world in which every map is reconfigured to suit the perspective of its user:

Now GPS puts me right at the centre,
A Ptolemaic shift in my perspective.

The term 'Ptolemaic shift' involves a wonderful paradox. We are familiar with the great 'paradigm shift' that occurred when we moved from the 'Ptolemaic' view of the universe, with the earth at the centre and the sun and stars moving round it in great crystalline spheres, to the 'Copernican' view of the universe with the sun at the centre and the earth and other planets orbiting round; this is referred to as the Copernican revolution or the Copernican shift. But here Ordway is suggesting that ironically the invention of hi-tech satnav has resulted instead in a Ptolemaic shift, in which we have put ourselves back in the centre of all the maps!

There is also a telling wordplay in her use of the word 'pinned':

Pinned where I am, right now, somewhere, I turn
And turn to orient myself.

Users of handheld GPS systems on their smartphones will be familiar with the idea of 'dropping pins' to mark their location or the location they are looking for as an aid to navigation, but 'pinned where I am' also carries the sense of being pinned down or trapped. We are accustomed to the sight of people whose eyes are fixed and pinned down on their smartphones as they walk, bumping into others and missing both the beauty and the clear landmarks of the world around them, and this is where the final 'turn' or 'volta' of the poem comes:

I have
Directions calculated, maps at hand:
Hopelessly lost till I look up at last.

'The map is not the reality,' as the old Zen Masters used to say. We can get lost in our representations, we can mistake the image for the real thing; sometimes we just have to look up and be where we are in order to see where that is. This certainly applies to our Christian pilgrimage. It is very helpful to have the images, ideas, maps and drawings of other Christians to help us on our journey – that is what tradition and community are for – but in the end it is no substitute for personal encounter and real presence, for looking up and being where we are with Christ.

Perhaps this is a good stage in our journey through Lent to look up and take stock, to keep to hand and use what is clear and helpful and to leave behind what is confusing or disorienting in the maps we have been given. Playing again on the idea of the turn or 'volta', Ordway offers us the image of someone turning and turning to orient themselves. But of course the word 'turn' has a deeper Christian resonance. The true turn, the real 'volta', is the turn we took at the beginning of this journey, on Shrove Tuesday and Ash Wednesday, the turn of metanoia or repentance, when we turned away from sin and turned to follow Christ. Every so often we should look up; if we have inadvertently turned and gone astray, we need to turn again and be 'oriented' to face again the true east of our rising sun!

sometimes you don't need to use Electronics to help you find your way. Ask God to help you. Also, Look around you and see the beauty God has made for us.

FRIDAY

The Song of Wandering Aengus *W. B. Yeats*

I went out to the hazel wood,
Because a fire was in my head,
And cut and peeled a hazel wand,
And hooked a berry to a thread;

And when white moths were on the wing,
And moth-like stars were flickering out,
I dropped the berry in a stream
And caught a little silver trout.

When I had laid it on the floor
I went to blow the fire a-flame,
But something rustled on the floor,
And someone called me by my name:

It had become a glimmering girl
With apple blossom in her hair
Who called me by my name and ran
And faded through the brightening air.

Though I am old with wandering
Through hollow lands and hilly lands,
I will find out where she has gone,
And kiss her lips and take her hands;

And walk among long dappled grass,
And pluck till time and times are done
The silver apples of the moon,
The golden apples of the sun.

We may go on pilgrimage, or wander in the wilderness in pursuit of a vision, but it is also usually the glimpse of a vision, the apprehension of 'something more', the half-heard voice, that seems to call to us in the first place and start us on our journey. Yeats' 'Song of the Wandering Aengus' expresses this perfectly for me. Taken from *The Wind Among the Reeds*, published in 1899, it represents for some the apotheosis of the poet's 'Celtic Twilight' period, but it expresses universal themes and experiences and transcends its original setting. Indeed it has been set to music by an array of contemporary musicians. There are many cycles of legends about Aengus, a god of love, youth and beauty, and in some of these stories he finds the girl again, transformed into a swan, and himself becomes a swan and they fly and sing together. But this is not how Yeats chooses to treat the story. For Yeats, Aengus represents perhaps not just the poet but every questing soul, and he is the one who retains his vision in spite of never, in this life, having it completely fulfilled. So Yeats has given us a poem not only about vision, yearning and love, but also about tenacity and clarity of vision, even into old age. I first read this poem as a young man, wondering around Ireland myself at the age of 19 on a full-blown romantic quest for truth and beauty that did not then find its fulfilment. I reread it now in middle age and each time I do it reconnects me with that first glimmering vision and questing heart of my youth, which has since begun to find its fulfilment in the beauty of the gospel, but still quests and yearns. For every Christian there is both a first vision and an unfulfilled 'not yet', and we must all say, in the words of another Irishman also indebted to Yeats, 'I still haven't found what I'm looking for.'

This whole poem has a musical, incantatory, magical quality, a sense of events unfolding as they must: the midnight visit to the wood, the cutting of the magic hazel wand, so associated with dowsing and water magic, and then the paradoxical turn on 'caught'. For the poet who thinks he has caught a trout has himself been caught, and will be drawn for the rest of his life on a line of desire and longing. The detail of the 'white moths on the wing' and, in pre-dawn, the 'moth-like stars flickering out' is particularly beautiful, and Yeats may here be recalling Shelley's haunting lines:

> The desire of the moth for the star,
> Of the night for the morrow,
> The devotion to something afar
> From the sphere of our sorrow.
> ('To ____')

For that is indeed the theme of his poem. Then comes the movement from 'something', to 'someone', and the key line of the whole poem: 'And someone called me by my name'.

Here we come to the heart and meaning of the word 'vocation'. A vocation is a calling, and to have a Christian vocation is to have been called, called by name. The Lord of life and love calls us out of nothingness into being, calls us out of darkness into light, and calls us, personally, to turn and begin our lives anew in him. All our lives, all our journeyings 'through hollow lands and hilly lands', are a response to that call. Our quest, like that of the wondering Aengus, begins at dawn and is an 'orientation': a turn towards the growing light. But this is not light as an abstract, it is light embodied in a person, and it calls to a vision and a realm beyond what is possible for us in this world. Yeats ends his poem with the mythically resonant image of

> The silver apples of the moon,
> The golden apples of the sun.

This evokes everything from the Garden of Eden to the gardens of the Hesperides, and also to me beautifully blends all that we mean at the deepest level by the sun and the moon. Emblematically and poetically the sun and the moon seem to embody the resonant and complementary pairing of elements within each of us, the masculine and the feminine, the reason and the imagination, the directly known and reflectively apprehended. In the last lines of this poem all these things are somehow brought together and offered as fruitful and beautiful for ever.

SATURDAY

First Steps, Brancaster *Malcolm Guite*

This is the day to leave the dark behind you
Take the adventure, step beyond the hearth,
Shake off at last the shackles that confined you,
And find the courage for the forward path.
You yearned for freedom through the long night watches,
The day has come and you are free to choose,
Now is your time and season.
Companioned still by your familiar crutches,
And leaning on the props you hope to lose,
You step outside and widen your horizon.

After the dimly burning wick of winter
That seemed to dull and darken everything
The April sun shines clear beyond your shelter
And clean as sight itself. The reed-birds sing,
As heaven reaches down to touch the earth
And circle her, revealing everywhere
A lovely, longed-for blue.
Breathe deep and be renewed by every breath,
Kinned to the keen east wind and cleansing air,
As though the blue itself were blowing through you.

You keep the coastal path where edge meets edge,
The sea and salt marsh touching in North Norfolk,
Reed cutters' cuttings, patterned in the sedge,
Open and ease the way that you will walk,
Unbroken reeds still wave their feathered fronds
Through which you glimpse the long line of the sea
And hear its healing voice.
Tentative steps begin to break your bonds,
You push on through the pain that sets you free,
Towards the day when broken bones rejoice

It's good that this call to journey and pilgrimage in Lent comes in the spring and the turn of the year. For many of us winter is dark and difficult. It was particularly so for me in the winter of last year as I coped with a broken leg. This poem, written to celebrate my first walk outdoors after the accident, alludes to Psalm 51, the great Lenten penitential psalm with its prayer to 'make me to hear of joy and gladness that the bones which thou hast broken may rejoice'.

The poem is set on the North Norfolk Coastal Path near the village of Brancaster and I hope it gives some sense of that wide, wild, bracing countryside. It is customary to speak of 'the pathetic fallacy', the habit whereby we project our inner feelings, our distinctively human 'pathos', onto the surrounding environment, so that the outward becomes expressive of the inward. But I don't think this is quite as fallacious as some people assume. The very fact that we find a constant and seemingly natural correspondence between the outer and inner may itself be a clue to the nature of the universe and our role in it. It may not be simply that we project, but that we, ourselves a part of nature, are finely attuned to and can give a conscious 'inward' expression to its outer meanings. Indeed, Coleridge went so far as to suggest that we are able to read the 'eternal language' which is already patterned into the appearances of nature. In his beautiful conversational poem 'Frost at Midnight' he imagines how his son, in opening himself fully to the experience and meaning of landscape, will

45

see and hear
The lovely shapes and sounds intelligible
Of that eternal language, which thy God
Utters, who from eternity doth teach
Himself in all, and all things in himself.
Great universal Teacher! he shall mould
Thy spirit, and by giving make it ask.

This is not the pantheism of which Coleridge is sometimes falsely accused. On the contrary, God transcends nature, which is not God himself but is his language. Certainly one sometimes can be aware of an outer scene entering deeply into one's soul as an expression of both consciousness and healing. This was my experience walking in Norfolk on the day commemorated in this poem. The lines that came first –

Kinned to the keen east wind and cleansing air,
As though the blue itself were blowing through you.

– came spontaneously as an expression of how that deep blue, keen air and wide horizon, after months of confinement, seemed somehow to change and expand my inward self. The walk itself was brief and painful, pushing myself with each step and leaning still on my crutches, but somehow also transformative. I include the poem here because the experience it describes seems to correspond with a real experience on most people's spiritual journey, a moment when vision is renewed; new possibilities become apparent even though we are still hobbled by our brokenness. That renewal is what gives us the courage to 'push on through the pain' in a strange and paradoxical combination of effort, grace and freedom.

WEEK 2

Deepening the Life of Prayer

SUNDAY

Postscript *Seamus Heaney*

And some time make the time to drive out west
Into County Clare, along the Flaggy Shore,
In September or October, when the wind
And the light are working off each other
So that the ocean on one side is wild
With foam and glitter, and inland among stones
The surface of a slate-grey lake is lit
By the earthed lightning of flock of swans,
Their feathers roughed and ruffling, white on white,
Their fully-grown headstrong-looking heads
Tucked or cresting or busy underwater.
Useless to think you'll park or capture it
More thoroughly. You are neither here nor there,
A hurry through which known and strange things pass
As big soft buffetings come at the car sideways
And catch the heart off guard and blow it open.

As we saw last week, all Sundays are exceptions to Lent for every
Sunday is a commemoration of the first day of the week, the
day of resurrection, and so really part of Easter. We should see
Sundays as little islands of vision in the midst of Lent. Last Sunday
we enjoyed R. S. Thomas' poem 'The Bright Field'; this poem of
Heaney's, which comes at the very end of his collection *The Spirit
Level*, is also about a moment of vision, and seems to me to be a
companion piece, perhaps gently alluding to 'The Bright Field'.

There are some extraordinary things going on in this poem. First there is the sheer vividness of its pictures: the ocean 'wild with foam and glitter', the 'earthed lightning' of the swans, the detail of

> Their feathers roughed and ruffling, white on white,
> Their fully-grown headstrong-looking heads
> Tucked or cresting or busy underwater.

Then there is the wonderfully evoked sound and feel of the wind that has ruffled the swans' feathers and lifted the foam of the sea, coming at the car 'As big soft buffetings' – an experience perfectly and vividly captured. In one sense the poem could not be more earthed and particular. Indeed, the vivid metaphor he uses for the way the brilliant white of the swans lights up the lake,

> The surface of a slate-grey lake is lit
> By the earthed lightning of flock of swans,

could serve as a metaphor for the whole poem, which is itself a kind of 'earthed lightning'. Earthed indeed, but for that very reason capable of conducting, like lightning, some power, some energy of light and also, almost, of danger. What that energy is comes through most powerfully in the final lines:

> You are neither here nor there,
> A hurry through which known and strange things pass
> As big soft buffetings come at the car sideways
> And catch the heart off guard and blow it open.

Suddenly we have moved from what is 'out there' to what is 'in here', and the poet turns to us directly and describes us unforgettably as 'a hurry through which known and strange things pass'. We are ourselves conductors! The strange beauties and energies of the world pass through us and it is up to us whether we are simply 'a hurry' through which they pass or if we might ourselves be changed and charged by what passes through us; in a phrase from another Heaney poem, be 'burnished by the passage'. Then comes that extraordinary final line with its use, and yet redemption, of the language of violence. So much of Heaney's earlier poetry, arising from the Troubles, had to be concerned with sudden violence, with cars parked by the side of the road to capture not a view but a victim, with people themselves being 'caught off guard' and 'blown open'. 'He was blown to bits out drinking in a curfew others obeyed,' Heaney wrote of one of his friends. And that is why this 'Postscript', this vision of the earthed lightening of the divine, is so telling and trustworthy. It speaks of the transition from 'the murderous' to 'the marvellous', to which Heaney pointed in his Nobel Prize acceptance speech:

> for years I was bowed to the desk like some monk bowed over his prie-dieu, some dutiful contemplative pivoting his under-standing in an attempt to bear his portion of the weight of the world, knowing himself incapable of heroic virtue or redemp-tive effect, but constrained by his obedience to his rule to repeat the effort and the posture. Blowing up sparks for a meagre heat. Forgetting faith, straining towards good works. Attending insufficiently to the diamond absolutes, among which must be counted the sufficiency of that which is absolutely imagined. Then finally and happily, and not in obedience to the dolorous circumstances of my native place but in spite of them, I straight-ened up. I began a few years ago to make space in my reckoning and imagining for the marvellous as well as the murderous.
> (*Opened Ground*, p. 458)

But here the transition is made through the redemption of lan-guage itself, as the very words once used to describe the murderous become the ones that open us utterly to the marvellous.

MONDAY

Prayer *George Herbert*

Prayer the Churches banquet, Angels age,
    Gods breath in man returning to his birth,
    The soul in paraphrase, heart in pilgrimage,
The Christian plummet sounding heav'n and earth;

Engine against th' Almightie, sinner's towre,
    Reversed thunder, Christ-side-piercing spear,
    The six daies world-transposing in an houre,
A kinde of tune, which all things heare and fear;

Softnesse, and peace, and joy, and love, and blisse,
    Exalted Manna, gladnesse of the best,
    Heaven in ordinarie, man well drest,
The milkie way, the bird of Paradise,

    Church-bells beyond the stars heard, the souls bloud,
    The land of spices, something understood.

Last week we were considering the idea of journey and pilgrimage as a way of thinking about Lent and about our spiritual lives more generally. This week I want to continue that theme but to add a particular focus. When we journey together we have time for thought and reflection, and if we have a companion, time for conversation, which can be sometimes rich and life-changing. Our journey through the chosen wilderness of Lent, indeed our wider journey through life, is a companioned journey. We are not alone. We have the friends and companions in this world and life who are making a similar journey, our comrades in the faith, we have the great cloud of witness, the saints who have walked these roads, completed the journey and from the shores of heaven encourage us in the walk of faith, and we have the Lord himself. Jesus fasted 40 days in the wilderness so that he could be with us on that journey. He came close to the sorrowing disciples on the road to Emmaus and asked them to share their grief so that eventually he could become known to them in the breaking of bread, and he comes close to us and asks us also to open our hearts. In these next two weeks I have chosen poems that help us reflect on that conversation with God and with one another, on the very nature of prayer itself, on the way we are companioned by the saints, and on our conversation with and encouragement of one another. We begin this week with a consideration of prayer as a kind of engagement and conversation.

One of the finest poems he wrote, George Herbert's 'Prayer' is a sonnet but not a sentence. Its richly laden 14 lines contain no fewer than 27 images or reflections of what prayer might be for us. From the uplifting 'exalted manna' to depth-sounding 'Christian plummet', from the heaven-ward ringing music of 'church bells beyond the stars heard' to the deeply incarnate discovery of 'Heaven in ordinarie', Herbert's imagery captures the ups and downs of our prayer life and maps out for us the spiritual terrain through which we are moving.

Our first impression is of the sheer wealth, almost over-abundance, of beautiful images contained in striking and memorable phrases we are being offered. This is not the honing and concentration on the single vision, but a kind of rainbow refraction of many insights, a scattering of broadcast seeds. For each of these images is in its own way a little poem, or the seed of a poem, ready to grow and unfold in the reader's mind. And the different seeds take root at different times, falling differently in the soil of the mind each time one returns to this poem. I have been reading it for over 30 years now and I still find its images springing up freshly in my mind and showing me new things. Let me take just two of the phrases here and open them up a little. I hope my readers will eventually do the same for all of them.

The opening phrase, 'Prayer the Churches banquet', carries with the choice of the word 'banquet' a picture not of some puritan modicum, a strict or grudging allowance of necessity, but rather of largesse, generosity, and the good measure of a royal occasion. It's a phrase that sets the poem's tone, for of course a *banquet* is exactly what Herbert gives us: course after course and layer after layer of nourishing images of the experience of prayer. But the phrase the 'Churches banquet' alludes to and summons up the rich and complex feast and banquet imagery in scripture and the Church's life. Behind this passage lies the covenant meal of the Old Testament, the great wedding feast with which Jesus so often compared the kingdom and to which we must bring ourselves 'well drest', but most importantly the Last Supper and through it Holy Communion, which is the foretaste of the banquet of heaven – to which, in another of Herbert's poems, Love himself bids us welcome.

> The six daies world-transposing in an houre,
> A kinde of tune, which all things heare and fear;

Transposition is very much what poetry and all literary art is about. To hear snatches from the huge unknowable symphony of experience, to catch them and transpose them to a key that resonates with our understanding, so that at some point they harmonize with that unheard melody from heaven we are always trying to hear, that is the purpose of poetry. 'Transposition' for Herbert in this poem involves taking the whole story of creation and reworking it within our individual life of prayer.

One might take each of these images in turn and find much fruit in them: the window on the mysteries of communion in 'exalted Manna'; all the sense both of life and sacrifice packed into 'souls bloud'; the evocation of the riches of the enchanted and faraway in 'land of spices'; and perhaps most tellingly the superb compression and paradox in 'Heaven in ordinarie', a phrase that in itself sums up the heart of the gospel in God's Incarnation in a stable, but also stands for the heart of the kind of poetry I have gathered together for this book.

TUESDAY

Homecoming *Gwyneth Lewis*

Two rivers deepening into one;
less said, more meant; a field of corn
adjusting to harvest; a battle won
by yielding; days emptied to their brim;
an autumn; a wedding; a logarithm;
self-evidence earned, a coming home
to something brand new but always known;
not doing, but being – a single noun;
now in infinity; a fortune found
in all that's disposable; not out there, but in,
the ceremonials of light in the rain;
the power of being nothing, but sane.

Herbert's 'Prayer' set something of a precedent, and a number of
other poets have tried their hand at this listing, incantatory mode
of poetry. The contemporary Welsh poet Gwyneth Lewis, strongly
aware of Herbert's own Welsh roots, has written in 'Homecoming'
a modern take on Herbert's poem. Her images speak both of our
awareness of meditation and mindfulness as part of the palette of
prayer and of the dangers of our overcrowded and assertive life-
styles, our need of 'days emptied to their brim' and battles 'won
by yielding'.

  As with 'Prayer', I would like to take just one or two of the
images she uses and open them out, leaving the reader the pleasure
of doing the same for all the rest. I start with the opening line:
'Two rivers deepening into one'.

There is something magical and exciting about a 'riversmeet' where two rivers join, often at the site of ancient human settlements. But the river itself, with its flow and movement on the one hand and its clear identity on the other, offers us a very good image of our own consciousness and identity. Heraclitus said, 'you can't step into the same river twice,' which is true in the sense that the very nature of its flow means that it is physically and particularly 'different water' every time you step into it. And yet its constancy of form makes us recognize that it is, in another sense, the same river. So it is with us. At every second the present flows into the past and the unknowable future arrives to become, for the fleeting moment, present. All we are is left behind, and yet received again. Gradually even the cells of our bodies change through death and renewal. They say that by the end of seven years every single cell is different, and yet we remain the same; our identity abides and, if we will let it, deepens.

And if we are to think of prayer or meditation as 'two rivers deepening into one' then we must think of that other greater river: the flow of God's loving, renewing and self-giving presence in the gift of his Holy Spirit. This is often presented as a rising fountain, a flowing stream, as in the promise Jesus gave to the Samaritan woman of a fountain rising within her to eternal life. We met this river in our very first poem when Heaney translated John of the Cross, the hidden fountain that is 'all sources' source and origin'. At any and every moment of prayer that river meets ours; they flow together, and then indeed in that union the channel of our own life, which might have been running shallow and babbling for a while, suddenly deepens.

But Lewis gives us more than just the traditionally poetic and spiritual image of the river. What, for example, are we to make of 'a logarithm'? This term seems suddenly to come from a different register, the dry world of mathematics, not the rich world of poetry, but if we look there are riches here too. Some of us are old enough to remember from pre-calculator days the 'log tables' we were given at school. For every number there was a transposed equivalent we could look up: a 'logarithm'. And the magic thing was that in the world of logarithms, hard and complicated multiplication became simple addition! You found the 'log' of the numbers you had to multiply, added them up, then when you transposed that figure back from logs to ordinary numbers, lo and behold, you had the right answer. I don't think I ever understood how that worked, but I remember being struck by how a transformation in one set of special terms somehow came up with a real answer in the terms I knew. Prayer, meditation and indeed the whole spiritual life are very like that. We may seem to leave the familiar and the everyday, we may work with Psalms, and symbols and sacraments that seem to come almost from another world, and yet, when we return to our 'ordinary life' after prayer, some questions have been answered, some solutions found. I think this is also what Herbert meant by 'the six days world-transposing in an houre'. Gwyneth Lewis has beautifully transposed his image from music to mathematics!

WEDNESDAY

Prayer/Walk *Malcolm Guite*

A hidden path that starts at a dead end,
Old ways, renewed by walking with a friend,
And crossing places taken hand in hand,

The passages where nothing need be said,
With bruised and scented sweetness underfoot
And unexpected birdsong overhead,

The sleeping life beneath a dark-mouthed burrow,
The rooted secrets rustling in a hedgerow,
The land's long memory in ridge and furrow,

A track once beaten and now overgrown
With complex textures, every kind of green,
Land- and cloud-scape melting into one,

The rich meandering of streams at play,
A setting out to find oneself astray,
And coming home at dusk a different way.

Continuing these reflections on the nature of prayer itself, I offer
another of my own poems, which, like Gwyneth Lewis' 'Home-
coming', is written in direct homage to Herbert's poem 'Prayer'.
I had come to notice that on retreats it was not always in the
'offices' in chapel but on walks and rambles in and around retreat
house grounds that I found the deepest spiritual renewal and the

best prayer. So I decided to write a poem that would be at once a celebration of walking in the countryside and of prayer itself. Every phrase in this poem is, I hope, an account of what walking is like and also an emblem of what prayer is like. As I have done with the previous two poems I will lift and open out one or two phrases and encourage my readers to do likewise with the rest. Take the first line, 'A hidden path that starts at a dead end'.

I have often noticed how interesting footpaths and bridleways start just beyond the brambles at the end of tarmacked roads marked 'dead end'. And it seems to me that this is very often where prayer starts too. I am sure that prayer should be a first resort, but it is sometimes the last resort when I've tried everything else! I've also noticed that the places in life where I get stuck and come up, as it were, against a 'dead end' sign are inevitably important places, where there is real stuff to deal with, and that is precisely why I get stuck or find it difficult to move forward. Too often we simply shy away from these personal dead ends and go for the first available diversion (usually Facebook!) to try something easier. But when I'm walking, the opposite is true. It gives me pleasure to explore the apparent dead end and find the hidden path where cars cannot go, to strike out across fields and leave the traffic behind, so I have tried to apply this to my prayer life. To begin the prayer at one of my personal dead ends and ask God to open up the path is a technique that has had some surprising and beautiful results!

> The sleeping life beneath a dark-mouthed burrow,
> The rooted secrets rustling in a hedgerow,
> The land's long memory in ridge and furrow,

You sense, on a good country walk, the hidden richness and depth of everything that is going on around you. You know that what you actually see – the close-up path ahead of you, the distant panorama, the occasional sweeping view of wider fields – are only a trace, a hint of what's really there. Suddenly you hear the hedgerow rustle or see the tracks of badgers or deer and you realize that you are walking among a whole web of life and exchange of which you are only partly aware. Again, features in the landscape itself suddenly speak of a long history and almost take you there. The ridges and ripples in a field you cross are remnants of the medieval 'ridge and furrow' agriculture, where your ancestors toiled on their separate 'strips' of soil, divided between the children of a large family. Again it seems to me that this experience is very true of our prayer life. When we begin to pray we have to start where we are, usually just on the surface of our lives; but there is always so much else going on. We all have a familiar outer layer to our lives but are there not also, deeper in our psyche, the burrows and dens where the shyer and more furtive elements of our inner life are rooted and nestling? Might these half-acknowledged parts of ourselves also be brought to God for blessing, noticed a little and offered to him? Do we have longer and deeper memories, perhaps going right back into our family histories, which have, as it were, shaped the landscape of who we are? Perhaps prayer, and particularly in Lent, might be a way to bring them for blessing and healing to God, for whom all times are present, in whom is the fullness of time.

Perhaps these last two poems, both responding to Herbert's 'Prayer', might encourage you to make a 'listing' poem of your own, filled with the images that have become, or could become, living emblems of your prayer life.

THURSDAY

How I talk to God *Kelly Belmonte*

Coffee in one hand
leaning in to share, listen:
How I talk to God.

'Momma, you're special.'
Three-year-old touches my cheek.
How God talks to me.

While driving I make
lists: done, do, hope, love, hate, try.
How I talk to God.

Above the highway
hawk: high, alone, free, focused.
How God talks to me.

Rash, impetuous
chatter, followed by silence:
How I talk to God.

First, second, third, fourth
chance to hear, then another:
How God talks to me.

Fetal position
under flannel sheets, weeping
How I talk to God.

Moonlight on pillow
tending to my open wounds
How God talks to me.

Pulling from my heap
of words, the ones that mean yes:
How I talk to God.

Infinite connects
with finite, without words:
How God talks to me.

We have talked about prayer as conversation on the journey, and
conversation has to be two-way. The contemporary American
poet Kelly Belmonte writes spare, simple verse, full of everyday
images, that goes right to the heart of the matter. This poem, 'How
I talk to God', is from her collection *Three Ways of Searching*.

It seems to me that this poem embodies, in a series of vivid
examples, what George Herbert called 'Heaven in ordinarie': there
is no special, 'sacred' location or church language in this series
of haiku-vignettes, and yet in every one of them the ordinary or
everyday is open to the sacred, and vice-versa, in every one, as the
concluding verse suggests, 'infinite connects with finite'. Though
she expands to the abstract words 'infinite' and 'finite' in her
conclusion, this is a wonderfully incarnate and particular poem,
rooted in the tactile and bodily: the coffee in hand, the touch on
a cheek from the toddler, the specifics of driving, the to-do lists,
the feel of flannel sheets. These are so much the usually unblessed
and unnoticed specifics of our lives, and there is grace in realizing
that every one of these is both the arena and the stuff of prayer.
The other distinctive thing in this seemingly secular poem is the
antiphonal feel, the sense of call and response in the alternating
refrain 'How I talk to God/How God talks to me'. This is prayer
not as closed monologue but as open exchange.

St Paul asks us to pray without ceasing, and some contem-
platives have understandably interpreted that as a call to leave the
world with its business and distractions and seek long swathes of

uninterrupted time devoted to prayer and prayer alone. Others have seen it as a call to have a continual hidden mantra, like the Jesus prayer, wheeling and cycling beneath all we do, providing an undercurrent or ground note of prayer beneath all our daily activities. Both these approaches have their merits and have proved fruitful in the lives of some of the greatest saints, but they are not for everyone. Most people don't have the opportunity or leisure, or the temperament or specific vocation, to detach themselves in that way; and yet in some sense continuous prayer remains a possibility. What this poem offers is a glimpse of how the very interruptions and mental preoccupations that sometimes clutter our days are themselves prayer if we will let them be, if we experience them in and with God. That first vivid image of leaning in to listen, coffee in hand, surely suggests someone not alone but in company, sharing coffee with a friend, on a 'break'; but that conversation turns out to be 'talking to God'. I love the way the first word from God in this conversational poem is through a three-year-old, utterly himself with his mother and yet also speaking God's word to her. 'Out of the mouths of babes and sucklings thou hast ordained wisdom'!

> While driving I make
> lists: done, do, hope, love, hate, try.

Again, these lines strike such a familiar chord, and are so honest and inclusive. Not just 'do' and 'try' but also 'love' and 'hate'. In 'Station Island XI', Heaney was advised to 'read poems as prayers'; here Belmonte models for us what it might mean to read 'lists' as prayers, to offer them to God, let him look at them and maybe make his emendations.

That unfiltered inclusiveness, there in the lists, is also in the movement in this poem from the highs of 'Momma, you're special' to the lows of lying curled up weeping in bed, and the way that in turn is followed by the midnight image of moonlight on the pillow and a God who tends to our 'open wounds'. Like Herbert's 'Prayer', this seems to be a poem whose beauty and simplicity of form invites us to 'go and do likewise'; to try our hand.

It may be that Belmonte's haiku sequence will encourage readers of this book to write down and remember those moments when the everyday is opened to the eternal.

make a list of
thoughts, feeling and
give them to God.
Let him deal
so that he can
help you.

FRIDAY

The Pains of Sleep *S. T. Coleridge*

Ere on my bed my limbs I lay,
It hath not been my use to pray
With moving lips or bended knees;
But silently, by slow degrees,
My spirit I to Love compose,
In humble trust mine eye-lids close,
With reverential resignation
No wish conceived, no thought exprest,
Only a sense of supplication;
A sense o'er all my soul imprest
That I am weak, yet not unblest,
Since in me, round me, every where
Eternal strength and Wisdom are.

But yester-night I prayed aloud
In anguish and in agony,
Up-starting from the fiendish crowd
Of shapes and thoughts that tortured me:
A lurid light, a trampling throng,
Sense of intolerable wrong,
And whom I scorned, those only strong!
Thirst of revenge, the powerless will
Still baffled, and yet burning still!
Desire with loathing strangely mixed
On wild or hateful objects fixed.
Fantastic passions! maddening brawl!

And shame and terror over all!
Deeds to be hid which were not hid,
Which all confused I could not know
Whether I suffered, or I did:
For all seemed guilt, remorse or woe,
My own or others still the same
Life-stifling fear, soul-stifling shame.

So two nights passed: the night's dismay
Saddened and stunned the coming day.
Sleep, the wide blessing, seemed to me
Distemper's worst calamity.
The third night, when my own loud scream
Had waked me from the fiendish dream,
O'ercome with sufferings strange and wild,
I wept as I had been a child;
And having thus by tears subdued
My anguish to a milder mood,
Such punishments, I said, were due
To natures deepliest stained with sin,
For aye entempesting anew
The unfathomable hell within,
The horror of their deeds to view,
To know and loathe, yet wish and do!
Such griefs with such men well agree,
But wherefore, wherefore fall on me?
To be loved is all I need,
And whom I love, I love indeed.

Kelly Belmonte gave us the image in 'How I talk to God' of
weeping and wakefulness:

Fetal position
under flannel sheets, weeping
How I talk to God.

Today I want to pursue that a little further and offer you a poem
that opens up questions about patterns and specifics of prayer and

also about the relation between the praying adult and the inner child (also hinted at in Belmonte's poem). It is well known that Coleridge struggled throughout his adult life with an opium addiction, originally acquired when he was being treated for agonizing pains in the knee at a time when little was known about the long-term addictive qualities of the opium-based cure-alls that were so widely and legally available in his day. Popular accounts have sometimes suggested that somehow the opium was all part of the romantic inspiration, but as Molly Lefebure has comprehensively demonstrated in her book *Samuel Taylor Coleridge: A Bondage of Opium*, nothing could be further from the case. Coleridge's brilliant achievements in writing were a fruit of heroic resistance to a drug which he knew was destroying his will and polluting the clear springs of his inspiration. One of the consequences of both the addiction and his many and prolonged attempts to be free of it, facing dreadful withdrawal symptoms, was draining bouts of insomnia and dreadful nightmares. Coleridge confronts these, and their relation to prayer, in the dark and searingly honest poem 'The Pains of Sleep'.

He starts off with an account of his 'bedtime prayers' not as formulaic repetition or particular intercession but as a kind of composed and open frame of mind, a 'reverential resignation'; not an actual prayer but rather 'a sense of supplication', and running through it all a diffused awareness that

in me, round me, every where
Eternal strength and Wisdom are.

This all sounds well and good and suggests perhaps the mature openness of someone who feels they may have grown beyond the childish lisping of their earlier forms of bedtime prayer, when they had prayed 'with moving lips or bended knees'. But at this point the poem suddenly turns and we realize that Coleridge's purpose is not to promote this vague and hazy spirituality but to reveal its utter inadequacy!

In the agonizing confession that follows he makes it clear that in confronting his demons and coming to the root of his (and our) wretchedness and fallenness, he needs to pray 'aloud in anguish and in agony'. Indeed he goes on later in the poem to reconnect with the inner child who had stopped praying in the old way: 'I wept as I had been a child'.

I have sometimes wondered, reading this poem, whether the strong rhythm and close rhyme of these four-stress lines is not a deliberate echo, a summoning, of the similarly strongly rhymed traditional child's prayer, which was well known in the late eighteenth century:

Now I lay me down to sleep,
I pray the Lord my soul to keep.
If I should die before I wake,
I pray the Lord my soul to take.

But if Coleridge needs to summon again the almost incantatory power of a child's remembered prayer, he does so because he must confront an adult's agony. One reason why Coleridge can speak very directly to our own age is that he lived in and confronted addiction, and its attendant self-loathing, which seems to be one of the deepest, if most hidden, curses of our time. In an age that should theoretically offer us greater possibilities of freedom than in any previous generation, we have in fact used that freedom to devise our own trammels and cages, and our entire culture of consumption seems designed at once to promote and conceal addictive and obsessive patterns of behaviour. The specifics of the addictions may have changed since Coleridge's day, but he fearlessly enumerates their real psychological and spiritual consequences:

The powerless will
Still baffled, and yet burning still!
Desire with loathing strangely mixed
On wild or hateful objects fixed ...
For all seemed guilt, remorse or woe,
My own or others still the same
Life-stifling fear, soul-stifling shame.

Even in the midst of this experience of chaos and depression Coleridge can see, though he cannot of his own power attain, what is needful, and he concludes this confessional cry in the night with a gesture towards love:

To be loved is all I need,
And whom I love, I love indeed.

In the end, like his Ancient Mariner, Coleridge did recover that capacity to give and receive love, and indeed returned to a full and profoundly held faith in Christ as the one, the only one, who could come down into the midst of his pain and set him free. He wrote some brilliant theology from the standpoint of that recovered faith, but it seems to me that it is his notes along the way, his frank cries of despair and longing, that can most help his fellow pilgrims now.

SATURDAY

Batter My Heart *John Donne*

Batter my heart, three-person'd God, for you
As yet but knock, breathe, shine, and seek to mend;
That I may rise and stand, o'erthrow me, and bend
Your force to break, blow, burn, and make me new.
I, like an usurp'd town to another due,
Labor to admit you, but oh, to no end;
Reason, your viceroy in me, me should defend,
But is captiv'd, and proves weak or untrue.
Yet dearly I love you, and would be lov'd fain,
But am betroth'd unto your enemy;
Divorce me, untie or break that knot again,
Take me to you, imprison me, for I,
Except you enthrall me, never shall be free,
Nor ever chaste, except you ravish me.

As we conclude this week's reflections on deepening the life of
prayer, we return to John Donne. He resolved the dilemma of
choice and discernment we encountered in 'Satire III', and com-
mitted himself fully to the Church of England, was ordained in
1615 and went on to become Dean of St Paul's and one of the
greatest preachers of his or any age. But this did not mean that he
ceased to wrestle with doubt or difficulty, with the riddling heart
or the contrary will, and continued to open the depth of these
issues in poetry of extraordinary power. *The Divine Meditations*,
from which this poem comes, were not published until after his
death, though they had been circulated in manuscript earlier,

and scholars disagree about the date of their composition. What is clear, however, is that for Donne, faith and prayer needed to involve the whole person and not just a pious set of behaviours and responses that form only one aspect of life. And therein lay the problem. Donne was aware that he was a highly complex, deeply conflicted person whose desires and interests, opinions and beliefs, pulled him in many different directions. Moreover he was immensely independent and strong-willed, while knowing and believing that at its heart his Christian vocation involved a renunciation of ego and a humility of which he felt scarcely capable. All this comes out in this poem in which he calls on God to take the active role, to step in and take over, in a dazzling series of vivid metaphors and paradoxes. He opens the sonnet abruptly and dramatically:

> Batter my heart, three-person'd God, for you
> As yet but knock, breathe, shine, and seek to mend;

Here the image is drawn from metalwork, and specifically the trade of the tinker – a bold metaphor for the work of God Almighty! It is as though he is a broken vessel that needs to be completely remade, beaten again into shape. It is not enough just to knock out the odd dent, to breathe on the copper and shine it up; Donne needs to be completely reworked. The effect of these short, sharp, kinetic verbs each pummelling in in the imperative voice is breathtaking: 'knock, breathe, shine ... bend ... break, blow, burn ... make'! But the end and purpose of it all is not to destroy but to 'make me new'.

Though these words were written 400 years ago many contemporary Christians will recognize Donne's dilemma and the necessity of this prayer, the need to be thrown down, to be knocked off one's perch, to be taken back to a beginning in order to start again with God.

In the next six lines Donne switches metaphors and draws his image from siege warfare, something he knew about first-hand as he had sailed with Raleigh and Sidney and taken part in the siege of Cadiz. But here he gives the metaphor a particular nuance: it is not a case of one people besieging another, as had happened between the English and Spanish. Donne compares himself to 'an usurp'd town to another due'. Here the besiegers are on the side of the true citizens! The town is being besieged not to be invaded by enemies but, on the contrary, to return it to its true sovereignty and oust the usurpers. Donne knows that God is his true sovereign; he knows that his own reason is, in a beautiful image, God's 'viceroy' in him. But somehow reason has been incapacitated, or has perhaps even rebelled and denied his sovereign. Donne typically allows an openness to both or either possibility; 'Reason ... is captiv'd, and proves weak or untrue'. But whatever the case, somehow the city of Man-soul, as Bunyan was later to call it, has been menaced by an internal *coup d'état*! Donne sees that in our state of unreason, incoherence and the bondage of the will we need God himself to come in and re-establish his place and his throne in our hearts. And at this point Donne makes a beautiful elision to a third metaphor: the struggle of human love and passion:

> Yet dearly I love you, and would be lov'd fain,
> But am betroth'd unto your enemy;
> Divorce me, untie or break that knot again,
> Take me to you,

Now it's personal. If the call to God to stop tinkering seemed too mechanistic, and the siege warfare too grandiose and impersonal, now we come to the heart of things and true intimacy. The quest to be reunited and 'right' with God becomes, paradoxically, the yearning away from the mere institution to the call of true love. In an age of arranged marriages, Donne himself had incurred the wrath of his patron and a term in prison for marrying for love; he knew what it was to have a true love frustrated and constrained by external forces. It is both daring and helpful to think of God as the secret lover for whom we yearn in spite of all the current institutional commercial and consumer forces – our arranged marriage to secularism – that try to keep us from him!

But there is one last turn to this sonnet. Donne was a famously passionate man and he knew that in fact this deepest of all passions, his love of God, would involve his learning to subdue, redeem and redirect the profound erotic energies of his being. For Donne this is not to be an icy renunciation, however, but rather the encounter with an even more overmastering passion, of which Eros himself might be only a shadow, and the poem comes to its celebrated and dramatic conclusion:

Except you enthrall me, never shall be free,
Nor ever chaste, except you ravish me.

WEEK 3

Dante and the Companioned Journey

Our theme for last week and also for this explores prayer under-
stood as conversation with God and with one another as fellow
pilgrims on the journey. In individual prayer, as we have seen, we
have many ways of hearing and speaking with God, but in our
wider spiritual life we are companioned and in conversation with
friends in both the here and now and the 'great cloud of witness'.
The poet who models that companionship most brilliantly, and
has been seen as a companion by many other poets, is Dante. The
whole of his poem the *Divine Comedy* is essentially an account of
a companioned journey: one that begins in solitude, finds a friend,
remembers a lost love and ends in divine Communion.

Because Dante is one of the 'great names', one of those authors
whose formidable marble bust might inhabit august library
alcoves, we tend to assume that his poem must also be formid-
able, but it is not so. Yes, he faces and guides us through the
horrors of Hell, but not in order to leave us there, and his poem
is at heart a celebration of love, human and divine, the love that
does not let us go!

It is essential to grasp that the poem is an allegory. That is to
say, while outwardly about the supposed fate of various souls in
the afterlife, it is really about who we are now, what we can still
make of ourselves, and how to travel on our own pilgrim road.
Dante's three realms of Hell, Purgatory and Paradise are really
maps of our own souls, souls that bear God's image. He shows
how the best in us can become darkened and destructive, but also
how it can be purged and redeemed, and finally how our capacity

for joy and wonder, for growing in light and love, will expand and deepen as we draw closer to the source of all light and love in the heart of God. In some ways Dante's central message is embodied in the very shape and structure of his journey through the three realms, which can be summarized very simply. Hell is a series of descending vicious circles, spiralling down into the self-obsession of the ego turned in on itself. So Dante's Satan is frozen at its icy centre, eternally consuming others but giving nothing. However, if we have courage to go past him then we reach the centre of the earth's gravity; then the world turns upside down and we climb again. Purgatory is a holy mountain, the positive shape that can be made of the negative pit of Hell. Here, though we have not escaped suffering, we can allow it to help and not hinder us: we spiral upwards, assisted by the prayers and companionship of the whole Church. Finally we return to Eden, remade and integrated as complete human beings, and from there we are drawn, with ever-expanding consciousness, into the heart of things, to Heaven itself, by a kind of upward gravitation of Love. For Dante the whole journey comes as a climax of Lent, taking place over the course of Good Friday and Easter!

During the course of this week I offer you three passages from Dante's great poem, and three poems that I have written in response to Dante as part of a sequence called 'On Reading the Commedia'. The Dante passages are in Robin Kirkpatrick's excellent new translation for Penguin Classics, which can be highly recommended both for its power as English poetry and for its very helpful commentary.

SUNDAY

Late Ripeness *Czeslaw Milosz*

Not soon, as late as the approach of my ninetieth year
I felt a door opening in me and I entered
the clarity of early morning.

One after another my former lives were departing,
like ships, together with their sorrow.

And the countries, cities, gardens, the bays of seas
assigned to my brush came closer,
ready now to be described better than they were before.

I was not separated from people, grief and pity joined us.
We forget – I kept saying – that we are children of the King.

From where we come there is no division
into Yes and No, into is, was and will be.

Moments from yesterday and from centuries ago –
a sword blow, the painting of eyelashes before a mirror
of polished metal, a lethal musket shot, a caravel
staving its hull against a reef – they dwell in us,
waiting for a fulfilment.

I knew, always, that I would be a worker in the vineyard,
as are all men and women living at the same time,
whether they are aware of it or not.

After the real struggles that Coleridge and Donne have shared with us we return to the notion that Sundays are an exception to Lent, that Sunday is always the day of resurrection. I offer another Sunday poem that is a glimpse of heaven, an opening door. Czeslaw Milosz's astonishing poem 'Late Ripeness', written in his nineties, is the last poem in his collected verse, and yet what the ageing poet sees and offers us is 'the clarity of early morning'.

Milosz, a Nobel Laureate and one of the great figures of our time (he died in 2004), lived through some of the worst episodes and most appalling atrocities of its history, as his early poem 'A Poor Christian looks at the Ghetto' makes clear. Having endured and survived the horrors of Nazi invasion, he then went on to witness and suffer from the oppression of their Communist successors, by whom he was eventually driven into exile, taking up residence in the United States. In later life he began writing original poetry in English as well as his native Polish, though he had also worked alongside and collaborated with many talented translators. Throughout such historical vicissitudes he remained both politically and socially engaged with the world but also constantly alert to the transcendent, the divine dimension, the moment of vision. A Catholic poet, both in the formal sense of his confessional adherence and also in the wider sense of his breadth and inclusiveness of vision, Milosz was a constant 'contra' to the secularism of our age and an inspiration to many other poets, not least Seamus Heaney. Far from resting on his laurels, he continued writing into old age to hone his craft, producing delicately wrought poems to clarify the vision and offer phrases to feed the souls of his readers.

'Late Ripeness' is just such a work. 'I entered the clarity of early morning' is not only an account of the poet himself but an invitation to the reader to walk through the door the poet felt 'opening in me'. The departing 'former lives' are not, I think, the imagined former lives of some reincarnation, but rather the accumulated layers of the many lives we all live, wrapped around one another and crammed into one lifetime. But in this poem they are disentangled and let go, 'departing, like ships, together with their sorrow'. And this clearing, or opening, is not a preparation to face nothingness or death, as it might have been with a poet such as, for example, Philip Larkin, but rather a readying and steadying of the mind for new work, as everything that has been, in his lovely phrase, 'assigned to my brush' comes closer. It's worth reflecting on the idea that certain things and certain things only have been 'assigned to our brush', given to us to work with, know and describe. It reminds me strongly of the Prayer Book petition that we should 'do all such good works as thou hast prepared for us to walk in'. Most of us are under pressure, external and internal, to do everything, be good at everything, be accountable to everyone for everything! It is not so. In the divine economy each of us has a particular grace, gift and devotion. Finding out what that is, and learning how to be guilt-free about not doing everything else, may be part of what our Lenten journey is for.

Having made this point about how individual and particular each vocation is, Milosz immediately goes on to express its complementary counterpoint – our connectedness and solidarity with one another:

I was not separated from people, grief and pity joined us.
We forget – I kept saying – that we are children of the King.

And again, at the end of the poem, he emphasizes the same idea with an allusion to Jesus' parable of the workers in the vineyard:

I knew, always, that I would be a worker in the vineyard,
as are all men and women living at the same time,
whether they are aware of it or not.

Like many of the poems we have encountered so far, 'Late Ripeness' works off an interplay and mutual illumination between heaven and earth. Though it is full of loving attention to the things of this world; 'cities, gardens, the bays of seas ... the painting of eyelashes ... a caravel', all these things are evoked not only in themselves but in the light of heaven, in the light of our being 'children of the King', in the knowledge that

From where we come there is no division
into Yes and No, into is, was and will be.

Though this is clearly a serene poem of explicit faith, it ends with
praise and compassion for those who do not share that faith, with
the calm understanding that all these things are true, and we are
working in our Father's vineyard whether we are 'aware of it or
not'. He does not judge the unaware, even as his poem offers them
a pathway into awareness.

MONDAY

Meeting Virgil *Dante*

'There is another road'

As I went, ruined, rushing to that low,
there had, before my eyes, been offered one
who seemed – long silent – to be faint and dry.
    Seeing him near in that great wilderness,
to him I screamed my *'miserere'*: 'Save me,
whatever – shadow or truly man – you be.'
    His answer came to me: 'No man; a man
I was in times long gone. Of Lombard stock,
my parents both by *patria* and Mantuan.
        And I was born, though late, *sub Iulio*.
I lived at Rome in good Augustus' day,
in times when all the gods were lying cheats.
    I was a poet then. I sang in praise
of all the virtues of Anchises' son. From Troy
he came – proud Ilion razed in flame.
    But you turn back. Why seek such grief and harm?
Why climb no higher up at lovely hill?
The cause and origin of joy shines there.'
    'So, could it be', I answered him, (my brow,
in shy respect bent low), 'you are that Virgil,
whose words flow wide, a river running full?
    You are the light and glory of all poets.
May this serve me: my ceaseless care, the love
so great, that made me search your writings through!

You are my teacher. You, my lord and law.
From you alone I took the fine-tuned style
that has, already, brought me so much honour.
  See you there? That beast! I turned because of that.
Help me – your wisdom's known – escape from her.
To every pulsing vein, she brings the tremor.
  Seeing my tears, he answered me: 'There is
another road. And that, if you intend
to quit this wilderness, you're bound to take.'
(*The Divine Comedy*, 'Inferno', lines 61–93)

Dante's poem opens 'At one point midway on our path of life', when he has lost his way in a dark wood. Like Herbert and Donne, he sees a hill he knows he must ascend but is driven back by three fearful beasts, which are of course embodiments of his own sins and dislocations. He is running fearfully from a she-wolf when he catches sight of the person who will be his chief guide and companion for the first two stages of his journey, and will teach him profound wisdom. In a daring move on Dante's part it turns out that this vital companion is not even a fellow Christian but is the pagan poet Virgil! The inspiration for this anthology is the conviction that there are poets who can be more than titles on our bookshelves, who can rise up, meet us and help us on our way. It is Virgil who reveals to Dante the profound truth, later echoed by John of the Cross and T. S. Eliot: 'The way down is the way up.' He (and we) must have the courage to descend and face the worst, in ourselves as well as others, if we are to come at last to our heavenly home. But, as we shall see, even in that descent we continually see signs that our Saviour has gone before us.

Our first extract comes not from the very opening of the poem but at the wonderful moment when, lost, perplexed and frightened, Dante suddenly realizes who has joined him on the road. Virgil introduces himself, and refers to his great poem, *The Aenead*, in a rather round-about way, but there is a reason for that.

I sang in praise
Of all the virtues of Anchises' son.

By referring to Aeneas, the hero of his poem, as 'Anchises' son' Virgil is gently reminding Dante of the passage, in Book 6 of the *Aenead*, in which Aeneas is given permission to descend into the underworld and have a powerful encounter with his father Anchises, which will help Aeneas understand his own purpose and mission, and keep him true on his long journey. And so it will be with Dante. 'Don't worry,' Virgil is saying, 'we will be going into the dark together, but I know the way there and I know the way back, and like the hero of the poem you love, you are going to have some life-changing encounters in my company!'

Dante's first encounter with Virgil is justly famous, and readers of C. S. Lewis' *The Great Divorce* will recognize how closely his own encounter with George Macdonald, of whom Lewis could say, 'You are my teacher. You my lord and law,' is modelled on this passage. But all of us probably have one particular writer we could describe as 'the one who has most found, most helped, most guided me.' For some it will be C. S. Lewis; for me it has been two very different poetic companions, one of them Dante, the other Coleridge. If you have such an author in your life, doubtless you have fantasized about meeting them and telling them how you feel, even if they lived in another age and wrote in another language. Dante realizes that fantasy and models it for us here.

Notice two essential things here: first, the things Dante most loved in Virgil, and praises him for, are the very things he will encounter in their fullness in Heaven. Dante says that in Virgil's poetry 'words flow wide, a river running full', and that Virgil is 'the light and glory of all poets'. Those two images, the flowing river and the glory of light, are the key elements in the 'Paradiso', where indeed, having left Virgil behind, Dante says, 'I saw light as a flowing river'. It may be that hidden in the poets and writers we love best is a vital clue about the heaven we are aiming for; that we should stay with and return often and with confidence to those lines and images that have most inspired us, even from our childhood.

Second, we should notice Virgil's reply. He brushes off Dante's praise as a matter of no importance, and gets straight down to teaching him a new and essential truth; he's on the wrong road, and he needs to take the right one. Again, this seems to be an important insight, and helps us to recover what great literature is really for. It's not an exclusive cultural acquisition, a badge of educated status, or something on which academics can hang their displays of erudition. It is there, in the words of Philip Sidney's *Defence of Poetry*, 'to delight and instruct'. First and foremost it delights, as I hope all the poetry in this anthology will do, and then it leads to truth, teaching us something worth knowing. It could be said that both of these simple aims have been lost sight of in our age. Here is a chance to restore them.

TUESDAY

Through the Gate *Malcolm Guite*

Begin the song exactly where you are,
For where you are contains where you have been
And holds the vision of your final sphere.

And do not fear the memory of sin;
There is a light that heals, and, where it falls,
Transfigures and redeems the darkest stain

Into translucent colour. Loose the veils
And draw the curtains back, unbar the doors,
Of that dread threshold where your spirit fails,

The hopeless gate that holds in all the fears
That haunt your shadowed city, fling it wide
And open to the light that finds, and fares

Through the dark pathways where you run and hide,
Through all the alleys of your riddled heart,
As pierced and open as his wounded side.

Open the map to him and make a start,
And down the dizzy spirals, through the dark,
his light will go before you. Let him chart

And name and heal. Expose the hidden ache
To him, the stinging fires and smoke that blind
Your judgement, carry you away, the mirk

And muted gloom in which you cannot find
The love that you once thought worth dying for.
Call him to all you cannot call to mind.

He comes to harrow Hell and now to your
Well-guarded fortress let his love descend.
The icy ego at your frozen core

Can hear his call at last. Will you respond?

So Dante begins again, accompanied by Virgil, and they come
to the very gate of Hell, with its famous inscription, 'Abandon
Hope All Ye Who Enter Here'! But they don't abandon hope, and
that is the whole point. It is hope that leads and draws them on;
hope inspired by love. For Virgil has revealed to Dante that it is
Beatrice, the woman with whom he had fallen so completely in
love as a young man, now in the bliss of Heaven, who has herself
'ventured down the dark descent' (to borrow Milton's phrase)
to find Virgil and ask for his help in rescuing Dante, so that she
and Dante can meet again and rise together through the spheres
of Heaven. Like Jesus, who went to the cross not for pain in itself
but 'for the joys that were set before him', so we are to make this
journey through the memories of pain and darkness, not to stay
with these things but to redeem them and move beyond them. And
the journey is itself made possible because Christ himself has gone
before: 'He descended into Hell.' Throughout the journey into the
Inferno we are shown signs that Christ has been this way ahead
of us and broken down the strongholds. Dante is here alluding to
one of the great lost Christian stories, which we need to recover
today: 'The Harrowing of Hell'. We, who build so many hells on
earth, need to know that there is no place so dark, no situation so
seemingly hopeless, that cannot be opened to the light of Christ
for rescue and redemption.

This is the theme I had in mind in writing this poem, which is
my 'reader response' to Dante's journey. Throughout I have been
mindful that the Inferno is really 'in here and right now' not 'out
there and back then', and emphatically not, if we trust in Christ,

some inevitable end awaiting us. In that knowledge we must have the courage to expose our own personal hells to Christ and let him harrow them with us, and that is precisely what Dante's great poem allows us to do. The great statesman and Dante enthusiast, W. E. Gladstone, said: 'The reading of Dante is not merely a pleasure, a tour de force, or a lesson; it is a vigorous discipline for the heart, the intellect, the whole man.'

For all of us, somewhere within, there is a threshold or a gate beyond which we feel we dare not go, but it may be just past that threshold that our real healing and restoration needs to take place. Sometimes the best way to get through that gate, and let Christ in, is a companioned inner journey, with a trusted 'soul friend' – a spiritual director or a priest to whom we can make confession in complete confidence. I have deliberately echoed the phrase from the form of confession, 'all I cannot call to mind', as a way of suggesting that this journey with Dante down the dark spirals, one sin leading to another, one wound inflicting the next, can itself be an invitation to confession, and so to absolution and release.

WEDNESDAY

Towards a Shining World *Dante*

Dante and Virgil emerge from hell and begin the ascent of Mount Purgatory.

So now we entered on that hidden Path,
my Lord and I, to move once more towards
a shining world. We did not care to rest.
We climbed, he going first and I behind,
until through some small aperture I saw
the lovely things the skies above us bear.
Now we came out, and once more saw the stars.
...

To race now over better waves, my ship
of mind – alive again – hoists sail, and leaves
behind its little keel the gulf that proved so cruel.
And I'll sing, now, about the second realm
where human spirits page themselves from stain,
becoming worthy to ascend to Heaven.
Here, too, dead poetry will rise again.
For now, you secret Muses, I am yours ...

Dawn was defeating now the last hours sung
by night, which fled before it. And far away
I recognised the tremblings of the sea.
Alone, we walked along the open plain,
as though, returning to a path we'd lost,
our steps, until we came to that, with vain.

Then, at a place in shadow with the dew
still fought against the sun and, cooled by breeze,
had scarcely yet been send out into vapour,
    my master placed the palms of both his hands,
spread wide, likely and gently on the tender grass.
And I, aware of what his purpose was,
    offered my tear-stained cheeks to meet his touch.
At which, he made once more entirely clean
the colour that the dark of Hell had hidden.
(*The Divine Comedy*, 'Inferno', lines 133-end; 'Purgatorio',
lines 1-8 and 115-29)

I have chosen, for this extract on the middle day of the middle
week of our journey through Lent, one of the great moments
of transition in Dante's poem, one that resonates with our own
moments of transition. It is the 'exit' that corresponds with the
dreadful gate through which we had to enter at the start of our
'Dante week'. And it is in this passage that Dante reveals one of
the deep purposes of poetry.

We start with the very last lines of the 'Inferno'. Having been
through Hell together, Dante and Virgil suddenly find them-
selves ascending, even though from Dante's point of view they
haven't changed direction! Here Dante has made brilliant meta-
phorical use of a simple piece of science, as well known then as
it is now. Dante knew that the earth is a sphere whose centre of
gravity will be at its exact physical centre. So he knew that if you
descended down and down, right to the earth's core, and then just
kept going, your world would be turned upside down! Without
changing direction you would suddenly be ascending up from that
core. He had asked us to imagine Hell as a narrowing pit going
down to the centre of the earth, and had placed Satan in all his
self-aggrandizing 'magnificence' as actually stuck in the core, like
a worm in the centre of an apple. So suddenly this proud, raven-
ing spirit is seen for what he really is; a fool stuck upside down
with his legs waving in the air! At last they can leave him behind
and climb back to the lovely things of our world: the sky and the
clear-shining stars. Hell itself, indeed all evil, is in truth just a

hideous inversion of the primal good things, and our repentance – our new beginning and redemption – is just a matter of turning things the right way up again. The world, fixated on the follies of ego and power, accused the first Christians of 'turning the world upside down' but in truth, says Dante, they were really turning things the right way up again! There is a spiritual and psychological truth for us here: if we can just keep going, and not lose hope in the midst of our own descent, we too may discover that 'the way down is the way up'.

So Dante and Virgil emerge at last, under the clear-shining stars, and all their powers and hopes revive. As Dante says at the very beginning of his second book, 'Purgatorio':

Here, too, dead poetry will rise again.
For now, you secret Muses, I am yours …

The two poets emerge onto a beautiful little island in the 'Antipodes', on the other side of the world, and there Virgil, seeing Dante's face stained with tears and smeared with the grime of Hell, does a very touching thing. He stoops down and washes Dante's face with the clear morning dew.

Seamus Heaney was very attracted to this passage and used it twice in his poetry as a way of talking about what poetry itself can do for us, which is indeed what Dante intended this passage to mean in his allegory. In 'The Strand at Lough Beg', an elegy for Colum McCartney, his cousin who was murdered in the Troubles, he relocates this island scene, places it on the shore of his local Lough Beg, and imagines encountering his cousin just after the murder:

I turn because the sweeping of your feet
Has stopped behind me, to find you on your knees
With blood and roadside muck in your hair and eyes,
Then Kneel in front of you in brimming grass
And gather up cold handfuls of the dew
To wash you, cousin. I dab you clean with moss
Fine as the drizzle out of a low cloud.
(*Opened Ground*, p. 153)

In a later poem, 'Station Island VIII', Heaney wondered whether this beautiful passage was a kind of evasion, and whether he had 'saccharined' his cousin's death 'with morning dew'. There is a danger, of course, that poetry and the arts can be perverted and used merely to mask and evade pain, and all poets tend to be alert to that danger; but I think Heaney's first instinct was right. When poetry has done its important work of revealing and describing the hidden hell we carry and perpetuate, it also has this power and privilege to cleanse and renew our vision, and set us on the right road again.

THURSDAY

De Magistro *Malcolm Guite* of the teacher

I thank my God I have emerged at last,
Blinking from Hell, to see these quiet stars,
Bewildered by the shadows that I cast.

You set me on this stair, in those rich hours
Pacing your study, chanting poetry.
The Word in you revealed his quickening powers,

Removed the daily veil, and let me see,
As sunlight played along your book-lined walls,
That words are windows onto mystery.

From Eden, whence the living fountain falls
In music, from the tower of ivory,
And from the hidden heart, he calls

In the language of Adam, creating memory
Of unfallen speech. He sets creation
Free from the carapace of history.

His image in us is imagination,
His Spirit is a sacrifice of breath
Upon the letters of his revelation.

In mid-most of the word-wood is a path
That leads back to the springs of truth in speech.
You showed it to me, kneeling on your hearth,

You showed me how my halting words might reach
To the mind's maker, to the source of Love,
And so you taught me what it means to teach.

Teaching, I have my ardours now to prove,
Climbing with joy the steps of Purgatory.
Teacher and pupil, both are on the move,

As fellow pilgrims on a needful journey.

Many of us can probably point to a figure like Virgil in our lives –
if not an author, perhaps a living friend and teacher who meets us
at the right moment, sets us on a good path and guides us on our
journey. In this poem I celebrate someone who did that for me: the
teacher, in fact, with whom I first read Dante. My poem takes its
point of departure from the moment of transition we considered
in Wednesday's end of the 'Inferno', when the poets emerge at
last from the dark and see again the sky and stars, and prepare to
begin the painful and yet joyful ascent of Mount Purgatory.

Again and again I find Dante's poem gives me glimpses both
of places I have been and of places I may well yet find myself;
in doing so it gives me a map, and with the map a way forward.
When I wrote this poem I was emerging from a period of depres-
sion. I was grateful to be past the worst but I realized that I had
work to do, things to redeem, an ascent to make. To do so I had to
call to mind all the resources available to me, and I found myself
summoning the powers of the poetry I had read, the insights and
example of the teachers who had guided me, and above all con-
centrating, as they had done, on the joyful task of teaching itself.
The title of this poem, 'De Magistro', means 'of the teacher'; it
is also the title of a little book by St Augustine, co-written as
a dialogue with his beloved son Adeodatus. Augustine tells how
father and son explore together what it means to learn and to
teach, and come to the conclusion that at any moment when we
suddenly 'recognize' a truth, and make a glad, inner assent to it,
it is not the outward and visible teacher, the person in the room,
who is the ultimate source of that truth and that assent, but rather

an 'inner' teacher, deep within us, a source of light and truth to whom we have brought each proposition for confirmation. That teacher, says Augustine, is Christ himself, the Logos, the Word in each of us, who guides us through the wilderness. At such moments of joyful recognition both teacher and pupil discern the Word in and through one another, and in and through the words they share.

Dante's poem begins 'in a dark wood' in 'midmost of the path of this life'. Sometimes words themselves can seem like a tangled wood, but a good teacher can show us the path, and guide us gradually to find the true source of all language and meaning in Christ the Logos. I have tried to evoke that experience in this poem:

> In mid-most of the word-wood is a path
> That leads back to the springs of truth in speech.
> You showed it to me, kneeling on your hearth,
>
> You showed me how my halting words might reach
> To the mind's maker, to the source of Love,
> And so you taught me what it means to teach.

Perhaps, in the midst of this Lenten journey, this is a good time to remember, give thanks and pray for those teachers, official and unofficial, through whom Christ has 'brought us safe thus far'.

FRIDAY

The Refining Fire *Dante*

Over my suppliant hands entwined, I leaned
just staring at the fire, imagining
bodies of human beings and seen burn.
    And both my trusted guides now turned to me.
And the Virgil spoke, to say: 'My dearest son,
here may be agony but never death.
    Remember this! Remember! And if I
led you to safety on Geryon's back,
what will I do when now so close to God?
    Believe this. And be sure. Were you to stay
a thousand years or more wombed in this fire,
you'd not been made the balder by one hair.
    And if, perhaps, you think I'm tricking you,
approach the fire and reassure yourself,
trying with your own hands your garment's hem.
    Have done, I say, have done with fearfulness.
Turn this way. Come and enter safely in!'
But I, against all conscience, stood stock still.
    And when he saw me stiff and obstinate,
he said, I little troubled: 'Look, my son,
between Beatrice and you there is just this wall ...'
    Ahead of me, he went to meet the fire,
and begged that Statius, who had walked the road
so long between us, now take up the rear.
    And, once within, I could have flung myself –

The heat that fire produced was measureless –
or coolness, in a vat of boiling glass.
   To strengthen me, my sweetest father spoke,
as on he went, of Beatrice always,
saying, 'it seems I see her eyes already.'
   And, guiding us, a voice sang from beyond.
So we, attending only to that voice,
came out and saw where now we could ascend.
   'Venite, benedicti Patris mei!'
sounded within what little light there was.
This overcame me and I could not look.
   (*The Divine Comedy*, 'Purgatorio', lines 16–32 and 46–60)

To reach this next extract, taken from near the end of the 'Purgatorio', I am flying you up to the very top of the mountain, to the circle of fire that guards the hidden Garden of Eden. Dante and Virgil, of course, have had to toil up the hard way, inch by inch and ledge by ledge, but on their way their load has been progressively lightened, and their lives been made clearer and more integrated. For in Dante's poem Purgatory is the realm not of the vicious circle but of the virtuous spiral! Though they go round in circles, as they did in Hell, they are going the other way now, ascending, and with every circle complete they meet an angel, at whose word and healing touch one after another of the seven capital sins is lifted from them. They started at the bottom of the mountain crushed, as we all are, by the heavy weight of Pride. For the very thing we think is exalting us up is really weighing us down; all that effort to keep up the image! Best to let it go and rest in humility, accepting that grace we all need. They have been through Envy, and learned to shut their eyes to the useless things we covet; they have stumbled through the black and blinding smoke of Anger; and so with the other sins, each thankfully left behind. But there is always something that stays with us, some besetting sin that, as Paul says, 'clings so close'. And so at last they come to the smallest circle, the least of the seven, but it still needs addressing. And that, as you will already have guessed, is Lust!

   Curiously enough, as they get close to where this particular sin is purged, and redeemed, the place seems to be full of poets! Indeed, Dante finally makes it through the fire in a kind of poetic conga, with Virgil forging ahead and the 'silver' Latin poet, Statius, bringing up the rear. And here we have to learn an essential truth. The *Divine Comedy*, and indeed our own spiritual life, is not about rejection, or suppression, it is about redemption. The circle of fire that surrounds Eden is, of course, an emblem of lust, of seemingly uncontrollable and burning desire, but it is also a symbol of divine Love: 'our God is a consuming fire'! The great art is to bring the one kind of flame into the holy presence of the other, so that it can be refined and become what it should be.

T. S. Eliot was especially drawn to this part of the *Commedia*, and alludes to it in the famous passage in 'Little Gidding' when the 'familiar compound ghost', whom he meets when he is fire-watching in the Blitz and is, in part, Dante himself, tells him that our pilgrim souls will always go 'from wrong to wrong' unless:

> restored by that refining fire
> Where you must move in measure, like a dancer.

That this 'refining fire' is emphatically not a rejection of Eros, that profound longing that kindles our deepest earthly loves, is made abundantly clear by the fact that it is the image of Beatrice, and the longing for her, that gets Dante through the fire. Indeed, we know perhaps even more than Dante did that this fire of Eros is an essential part of our energy as human beings. We must learn to embrace it and get it working on the side of the other virtues, not against them. Merely to repress or deny it is to invite the fire to break out destructively and unexpectedly in other parts of our lives. Here Dante's poem speaks in a surprisingly modern way about our need for wholeness and integration.

So Dante is drawn through the fire not only by Virgil's praise of Beatrice, whom he will meet beyond the flames:

> my sweetest father spoke,
> as on he went, of Beatrice always,
> saying, it seems I see her eyes already

but also by the sound of singing, by the warmth of voices in harmony:

> a voice sang from beyond.
> So we, attending only to that voice,
> came out and saw where now we could ascend.
>   '*Venite, benedicti Patris mei*!'
> sounded within what little light there was.

Once more, it is the human and imaginative arts – music, poetry, song – that are not rejected in some puritanical fearfulness but yoked with Christ called to our aid. And it is the words of Christ himself that these voices are singing, the great words of welcome at the end of Matthew's Gospel: 'Come, ye blessed of my Father'! The very words that Dante would have seen, coming from the mouth of an angel, in the mosaics of the Baptistery in Florence, when he was a little boy.

SATURDAY

Dancing Through the Fire *Malcolm Guite*

Then stir my love in idleness to flame
To find at last the free refining fire
That guards the hidden garden whence I came.

O do not kill, but quicken my desire,
Better to spur me on than leave me cold.
Not maimed I come to you, I come entire,

Lit by the loves that warm, the lusts that scald,
That you may prove the one, reprove the other,
Though both have been the strength by which I scaled

The steps so far to come where poets gather
And sing such songs as love gives them to sing.
I thank God for the ones who brought me hither

And taught me by example how to bring
The slow growth of a poem to fruition
And let it be itself, a living thing,

Taught me to trust the gifts of intuition
And still to try the tautness of each line,
Taught me to taste the grace of transformation

And trace in dust the face of the divine,
Taught me the truth, as poet and as Christian,
That drawing water turns it into wine.

Now I am drawn through their imagination
To dare to dance with them into the fire,
Harder than any grand renunciation,

To bring to Christ the heart of my desire
Just as it is in every imperfection,
Surrendered to his bright refiner's fire

That love might have its death and resurrection.

So, at the end of this 'Dante week', I give you my own poetic
response to Friday's passage from the 'Purgatorio'. And I take
occasion in this poem to thank God for the warm-hearted poets
whose strength, and yes, sometimes weakness too, was in their
service of Eros, but who always gave me, as the pagan Virgil
gave Dante, a new kindling of hope and longing: a vision, even
through the warmth of earthly love, of the eternal Love of heaven.
Through them I learned that the right response to Eros is to ask
not for less desire but for more, to deepen my desires until nothing
but heaven can satisfy them. I also explore here the art of poetry
itself. There is a parallel, I think, between our love-life and the
making of poetry. In both there is an initial gift and inspiration,
a subtle and all-transforming intuition of beauty. But in both this
might easily be frittered away or corrupted. The first glimpse, the
intuition, which (as it did for Yeats' Wandering Aengus) should
lead to a lifetime's quest, can be lost or dissipated in the pursuit
of one will-o'-the-wisp after another. Or we can be faithful to it:
that first intuition, that graceful gift of love, can be attended to
and shaped. We can craft for it a steady reliable form and a home.
We can bring it, in poetry and in love-life, through slow growth
to fruition. So I praise the poets, among them Dante himself, who

taught me by example how to bring
The slow growth of a poem to fruition
And let it be itself, a living thing,

And we can do more than that. Poetry must begin with specific and loving attention to the particular and the earthly, but it doesn't end there. And so I also praise the poets who

> Taught me to trust the gifts of intuition
> And still to try the tautness of each line,
> Taught me to taste the grace of transformation
>
> And trace in dust the face of the divine,
> Taught me the truth, as poet and as Christian,
> That drawing water turns it into wine.

The lines, the images, the sounds and rhythms of a poem are all physical things of this world, and yet somehow, in them and through them, another light shines. George Herbert put it perfectly in 'The Elixir':

> A man that looks on glass
> On it may stay his eye
> Or if he pleaseth, through it pass,
> And then the Heavens espy.

And all this that is true of poetry is also true of the transformation of Eros in our lives. The familiar face of the person we live with, the quality of their steadfast covenant love, can suddenly become a window through which the face of the God who loves us in and through them shines. Marriage itself is intended as the sacrament in which that transformation can happen, and that is why the marriage service alludes to our Lord's presence 'at a wedding in Cana of Galilee'. For the miracle that was wrought there, in which the very act of drawing water in Christ's presence has turned it into wine, is a sign of what can happen to all we love and make in this world, both poems and relationships, if we open them up to Christ.

WEEK 4

Know Thyself! A Conversation with Sir John Davies and Alfred Lord Tennyson

Last week we walked with Dante, and I now want to develop this sense of our 'companioned journey' by drawing alongside two poets who may help us with our reflections on the way. In particular I want to share with you some gems from their longer poems which, precisely because they occur in the midst of long poems, are very rarely anthologized, but they have a great deal to offer us. The twin themes that I hope these poets will open for us are self-questioning on the one hand and self-knowledge on the other. Anyone who has undertaken a long pilgrimage, or a journey such as we are doing through Lent, will know that there comes a time when, as other concerns subside, the big questions arise: Who am I? How much do I really know myself? What can I really know about God? How can I trust that knowledge?

Now doubt and faith are sometimes seen as opposites that exclude one another, but as I show through these poems, that is not really the case. Honest open questioning of ourselves and our assumptions sometimes issues not from the loss of faith but its deepening and maturity. As we shall see, it was Tennyson, in the midst of *In Memoriam*, a poem that explored real doubt and grief, who came to realize:

There lives more faith in honest doubt,
Believe me, than in half the creeds.

But I begin on Monday with the earlier and less well known of the two poets, Sir John Davies.

MOTHERING SUNDAY

Mothering Sunday *Malcolm Guite*

At last, in spite of all, a recognition,
For those who loved and laboured for so long,
Who brought us, through that labour, to fruition
To flourish in the place where we belong.
A thanks to those who stayed and did the raising,
Who buckled down and did the work of two,
Whom governments have mocked instead of praising,
Who hid their heart-break and still struggled through,
The single mothers forced onto the edge
Whose work the world has overlooked, neglected,
Invisible to wealth and privilege,
But in whose lives the kingdom is reflected.
Now into Christ our mother church we bring them,
Who shares with them the birth-pangs of His Kingdom.

Perhaps it is appropriate, following Saturday's reflection on the
fruition of earthly loves, that we come to Mothering Sunday!

For this fourth Sunday in Lent, sometimes known as Refresh-
ment Sunday, is also celebrated as Mothering Sunday. As society
has grown more secular Mothering Sunday has eventually become
'Mother's Day', but it is good to remember its rich roots and to
see how the celebration of God's nurturing care for us, the nurture
of our parents, and the church community as itself a place for
nurturing and growth are all essentially linked together.

The idea of the Church herself as mother to us is very ancient, and may go back to Jesus' own comparison of himself to a mother hen in Matthew 23.37:

> Jerusalem, Jerusalem, the city that kills the prophets and stones those who are sent to it! How often I have desired to gather your children together as a hen gathers her brood under her wrings, and you were not willing!

Perhaps more telling still are the references to 'the birth-pangs of the kingdom'. That recognition that God himself knows both the pain and the fruitfulness of labour and birth seems to me an essential element in Christianity. Indeed, there is a very striking passage in John's Gospel where Jesus asks the disciples to imagine that they themselves were pregnant and going through labour pains, and then that they have given birth, in order that they should understand both the time of trial that they will go through as his followers but also the fruitfulness of that discipleship for themselves and for the world:

> When a woman is in labour, she has pain, because her hour has come. But when her child is born, she no longer remembers the anguish because of the joy of having brought a human being into the world. So you have pain now; but I will see you again, and your hearts will rejoice, and no one will take your joy from you. (John 16.21–22)

This notion of both empathizing with the birth-pangs of others and sharing with God in the birth-pangs of the kingdom is something I particularly draw out at the end of today's poem.

Mothering Sunday is a festival that is still evolving; for me it seems a very good day to remember, pray for and support the many single parents in our society: the ones who have been abandoned or betrayed by their partner, the ones who have stayed to raise and care for children. So in my sonnet for this day of thanksgiving for all parents, especially for those who bore the fruitful pain of labour, I have particular praise for those heroic lone parents who for whatever reason have found themselves bearing the burdens on their own, sharing with no one the joys of parenthood. It's my prayer that the Church, the local Christian community, can become like a mother for those single parents and an extra parent for their children, so that they 'who have been in sorrow' may also 'rejoice with great joy'.

MONDAY

Why did my parents send me to the schools? *John Davies*

Why did my parents send me to the Schools,
That I with knowledge might enrich my mind?
Since the desire to know first made men fools,
And did corrupt the root of all mankind.

Even so by tasting of that fruit forbid,
Where they sought knowledge, they did error find;
Ill they desir'd to know, and ill they did;
And to give Passion eyes, made Reason blind.

For then their minds did first in Passion see
Those wretched shapes of misery and woe,
Of nakedness, of shame, of poverty,
Which then their own experience made them know.

But then grew Reason dark, that she no more,
Could the faire forms of Good and Truth discern;
Bats they became, that eagles were before:
And this they got by their desire to learn.

All things without, which round about we see,
We seek to know, and how therewith to do:
But that whereby we reason, live and be,
Within our selves, we strangers are thereto.

We seek to know the moving of each sphere,
And the strange cause of th'ebs and floods of Nile;
But of that clock within our breasts we bear,
The subtle motions we forget the while.

We that acquaint our selves with every Zone
And pass both Tropics and behold the Poles,
When we come home, are to our selves unknown,
And unacquainted still with our own souls.

We study Speech but others we persuade;
We leech-craft learn, but others cure with it;
We interpret laws, which other men have made,
But read not those which in our hearts are writ.

Is it because the mind is like the eye,
Through which it gathers knowledge by degrees –
Whose rays reflect not, but spread outwardly:
Not seeing itself when other things it sees?

No, doubtless; for the mind can backward cast
Upon her self her understanding light;
But she is so corrupt, and so defac't,
As her own image doth her self affright.

John Davies was a slightly younger contemporary of Shakespeare and his most famous poem, 'Orchestra', a real *jeu d'esprit*, was published in 1596, almost exactly the same time as the composition of *A Midsummer Night's Dream*, when Davies was 26 and Shakespeare was 30. The poem celebrates the whole cosmos as a great dance, led and orchestrated by Love! It is in many respects the work of a young man, full of a delight in punning, playful with ideas, and alternates an attractive combination of seriousness and mischief. But it is also a channel for the great ideas and images of Christendom, not simply those of Davies' own day but the whole integrated body of thought and feeling about ourselves and the world, which Lewis so beautifully describes and elegizes in *The Discarded Image*.

Davies followed 'Orchestra' with an equally brilliant and highly readable (though less well-known) poem called 'Nosce Te Ipsum'. A poem of nearly 2,000 lines, 'Nosce Te ipsum', which means 'Know Thyself!', takes its title from the famous words of the oracle at Delphi. It opens, paradoxically, by questioning why we should go to school or bother learning anything at all:

> Why did my parents send me to the Schools,
> That I with knowledge might enrich my mind?
> Since the desire to know first made men fools,
> And did corrupt the root of all mankind.

In this playful opening, Davies is actually employing a method known as *disputatio*, used by Aquinas among others, which is to begin any enquiry by expressing and acknowledging the force of the opposite point of view, taking this into account before enunciating one's own.

So Davies begins his poem, which is going to be a hopeful account of the possibility of acquiring real knowledge of the world and ourselves, by facing head on our 'fallenness' – the broken and conditional forms of our knowledge. After giving a pithy account of the Fall, Davies concludes that our fallen condition means that the relations between Reason and Passion in each of us have become disordered. Our failure to see the world as it really is results from our pursuit of an isolated egotism; however, the answer to this loss of insight is not to abandon Reason or to distrust learning *per se*. It is instead to realize that our knowledge of the world, especially when the appetite for power and exploration drives the search for it, is flawed and dangerous, both for the world and for ourselves. The missing element is self-knowledge:

> All things without, which round about we see,
> We seek to know, and how therewith to do:
> But that whereby we reason, live and be,
> Within our selves, we strangers are thereto.

What we need is the kind of self-knowledge that will lead us to understand that we are not self-made, that will put ourselves and our world into better perspective. Davies exclaims upon the strange paradox of our sophisticated knowledge of the world set against our wilful self-ignorance. Anticipating both Freud and Jung, he suggests that we prefer to hide ourselves rather than know ourselves, because we are afraid of what we might find:

> for the mind can backward cast
> Upon her self her understanding light;
> But she is so corrupt, and so defac't,
> As her own image doth her self affright.

The poet's response to this insight is not flight or cynicism – the two characteristic responses of our own age – but rather courage-ous exploration. Today we read verses from the opening of the poem, setting out the dilemma; in the next three days we will see some of the surprising and moving conclusions Davies came to.

TUESDAY

What It Is To Be Human *John Davies*

She within lists my ranging mind hath brought,
That now beyond my self I list not go;
My self am centre of my circling thought,
Only my self I study, learn, and know.

I know my body's of so frail a kind,
As force without, fevers within can kill:
I know the heavenly nature of my mind,
But 'tis corrupted both in wit and will:

I know my soul hath power to know all things,
Yet is she blind and ignorant in all;
I know I am one of nature's little kings,
Yet to the least and vilest things am thrall.

I know my life's a pain and but a span,
I know my Sense is mockt with every thing:
And to conclude, I know my self a man,
Which is a proud, and yet a wretched thing.

So, how are we to get past that reluctance of the mind to look in
on itself that Davies observed at the end of yesterday's extract, and
move on to some real self-knowledge? Later in the poem Davies
goes on to argue that it is only when we suffer affliction that we
are motivated to turn our attention in and ask serious questions
of ourselves. Otherwise we just fritter away our time in distrac-

tions, and let our 'ranging minds' go where they will, as long as it's not home to look at ourselves. But when things go wrong, when we are ill or confined to quarters and thrown back on our own resources, then the real questioning and the fruitful work can begin. Just before the passage we read today, Davies tells us in a playful parable that he has met with failure, disappointment and illness; all three are summed up in the word 'Affliction'. But in his poem Affliction appears not as a hag or a nightmare but as a wise woman teaching him what he needs to know, rather as Philosophy appeared to Boethius in his cell:

> She within lists my ranging mind hath brought,
> That now beyond my self I list not go;
> My self am centre of my circling thought,
> Only my self I study, learn, and know.

There is a lovely play on the word 'lists' here. Lists were set areas marked off for contenders in tournaments, but 'list' also meant 'to will', or want something strongly. Affliction curbs his 'list', or lust, for novelty and brings him into the lists for more concentrated contention with himself, leading to self-knowledge.

So the arrival of Affliction leads to one of the poem's great set-piece expressions of the ambiguities and paradoxes of being human. In a passage that anticipates Hamlet's 'What a piece of work is a man' speech, Davies constantly juxtaposes our greatness and our frailty, our extraordinary capacity and potential and our always besetting weakness, our heavenly nature and our constant corruption. But all the knowledge in this great passage comes to him because he has allowed himself to learn from Affliction, the wise woman.

WEDNESDAY

The Light which makes the light which makes the day
John Davies

That Power which gave me eyes the World to view,
To see my self infused an inward light,
Whereby my soul, as by a mirror true,
Of her own form may take a perfect sight,

But as the sharpest eye discerneth nought,
Except the sun-beams in the air doe shine:
So the best soul with her reflecting thought,
Sees not her self without some light divine.

To judge her self she must her self transcend,
As greater circles comprehend the less;
But she wants power, her own powers to extend,
As fettered men can not their strength express.

O Light which mak'st the light, which makes the day!
Which set'st the eye without, and mind within;
Lighten my spirit with one clear heavenly ray,
Which now to view it self doth first begin.

But Thou which didst man's soul of nothing make,
And when to nothing it was fallen again,
To make it new the form of man didst take,
And God with God, becam'st a Man with men.

Thou, that hast fashioned twice this soul of ours,
So that she is by double title Thine,
Thou only knowest her nature and her pow'rs,
Her subtle form Thou only canst define ...

But Thou bright Morning Star, Thou rising Sun,
Which in these later times hast brought to light
Those mysteries, that since the world begun,
Lay hid in darkness and eternal night;

Thou (like the sun) dost with indifferent ray,
Into the palace and the cottage shine,
And shew'st the soul both to the clerk and lay,
By the clear lamp of Thy Oracle divine.

Once he has allowed Affliction to concentrate his mind, Davies concludes that we cannot account for the world and ourselves unless we look beyond ourselves to a source, a maker both of ourselves and of the world in which we participate. We must begin by acknowledging the mystery of our own minds; we must cast back upon ourselves what Davies called in our first extract 'our understanding light'. In so doing, Davies believes, we will encounter another light, an 'understanding light' cast upon us from beyond ourselves and our world, a light that is at once the source of our consciousness and the source of the world of which we are conscious. Indeed, he realizes that unless there is another light, one that transcends us and yet is available to us, then we have no chance of really seeing ourselves. The key verse is where he says of the soul:

To judge her self she must her self transcend,
As greater circles comprehend the less;
But she wants power, her own powers to extend,
As fettered men can not their strength express.

One of the tragedies of our age, with its reductive, atomistic account of knowledge, is that we ignore or exclude that other light by which we are able to have consciousness at all. By contrast, Davies not only reflects on that necessary inner light, he comes to an extraordinary conclusion about it, and even gives it a name. He realizes that this transcendent light, which must exist as light in our souls as well as beyond them, is one and the same with the one who said, 'I am the light of the World'! It is not an abstract diffuse transcendent consciousness, but a personal and loving Saviour. For Davies, the discovery of a transcendent light is not only a solution to a philosophical problem of knowledge, it is a personal encounter with Jesus, the God who became man for us. He moves seamlessly from one to the other in a little-known passage that is one of the great moments in English poetry:

O Light which mak'st the light, which makes the day!
Which set'st the eye without, and mind within;
Lighten my spirit with one clear heavenly ray,
Which now to view it self doth first begin.

But Thou which didst man's soul of nothing make,
And when to nothing it was fallen again,
To make it new the form of man didst take,
And God with God, becam'st a Man with men.

Finally in this extract he appeals to the light of Christ as equally available to all people, breaking down the false barriers of class and wealth, and even the divisions between ordained and lay so prevalent in the Church in both his age and ours:

Thou (like the sun) dost with indifferent ray,
Into the palace and the cottage shine,
And shew'st the soul both to the clerk and lay,
By the clear lamp of Thy Oracle divine.

'Indifferent' here is a teasing echo of the petition in the Book of Common Prayer that those in power might 'truly and indifferently minister justice'. It does not mean 'indifferent' in the modern sense of 'couldn't care less'; on the contrary, it means 'with great diligence' and without 'difference' or prejudice, making something equally available to all. If God can do that with the light of day, and with the inner light of his presence, why can't we manage it in our common and political life?

THURSDAY

Death as Birth *John Davies*

The first life, in the mother's womb is spent,
Where she her nursing power doth only use;
Where, when she finds defect of nourishment,
She expels her body, and this world she views.

This we call Birth; but if the child could speak,
He Death would call it; and of Nature plain,
That she would thrust him out naked and weak,
And in his passage pinch him with such pain.

Yet, out he comes, and in this world is placed
Where all his Senses in perfection bee:
Where he finds flowers to smell, and fruits to taste;
And sounds to hear, and sundry forms to see.

When he hath past some time upon this stage,
His Reason then a little seems to wake;
Which, though the spring, when sense doth fade with age,
Yet can she here no perfect practise make.

Then doth th'aspiring Soul the body leave,
Which we call Death; but were it known to all,
What life our souls do by this death receive,
Men would it birth or gaol delivery call.

In this third life, Reason will be so bright,
As that her spark will like the sun-beams shine,
And shall of God enioy the real sight,
Being still increased by influence divine.

Acclamation

O ignorant poor man! what dost thou bear
Locked up within the casket of thy breast?
What jewels, and what riches hast thou there!
What heavenly treasure in so weak a chest!

Look in thy soul, and thou shalt beauties find,
Like those which drowned Narcissus in the flood:
Honour and Pleasure both are in thy mind,
And all that in the world is counted Good.

And when thou think'st of her eternity,
Think not that Death against her nature is;
Think it a birth: and when thou goest to die,
Sing like a swan, as if thou went'st to bliss.

Our final extract comes from the last part of 'Nosce Te Ipsum',
and amounts to a beautiful and hopeful meditation on death
which paradoxically begins and ends with the image of birth.
Here Davies begins by asking us to imagine birth from the point
of view of the babe in the womb, who knows only the world he
is leaving and nothing about the outside world into which he is
being born. From the baby's point of view this expulsion from
the familiar surroundings, and the severance of the umbilical cord
which is its source of life, would seem a prospect as fearful as
death seems to us, and for the same reasons. Davies goes on to
describe our growth in the new life to which we are born and the
awakening of Reason which, as we have seen, for him includes the
awakening of the spiritual and imaginative life. This can itself be a
preparation for the next departure and discovery, which is death,
reimagined for us by Davies as a new birth.

If you could talk to a babe in the womb and tell it what was about to happen at birth, it would quite understandably be fearful and say, 'No, thanks! I'm quite comfortable where I am. I don't want to lose everything I know!' And it would take a great act of faith for the babe to trust that far from losing the mother who has wombed him there in the familiar darkness, he is now embarking on a whole new adventure in which, at last, he will see that mother face to face! But first must come the trauma of birth.

And so it is with us when we contemplate the time when we will leave the womb of this world. Readers of this great passage may be puzzled by a strange and interesting thing going on with gender; Davies seems to alternate between 'she' and 'he' when he refers to the baby to be born. This is because when he talks of the body he is imagining a boy being born; when he uses 'she' he is speaking of the soul, which, as did everyone in his age, he understands as feminine. Something for us to ponder!

The whole poem ends with an 'Acclamation', appealing to us not to despise, marginalize or ignore the hidden spiritual dimension of our life, this light that pervades the atmosphere of our bodies. It is as though Davies could predict the coming disaster of reductionism, could foresee the modern consumerist world into which we have been born: a world in which no one is credited with a soul, everyone is analysed in terms of complexes and chemicals and valued only as a potential consumer. It is a world where no meaning or value is given us or lasts for ever, where we choose not between eternal destinies but between lifestyle options, where we compensate for our meaninglessness and poor self-esteem with sex and shopping; but we still despair when death comes. Davies stands at the threshold of that modern world, but still carrying the spiritual insights of the ancient world, its symbols and its courtesies in every fibre of his being.

FRIDAY

Faith in Honest Doubt *Alfred Tennyson*

You tell me, doubt is Devil-born.

I know not: one indeed I knew
In many a subtle question versed,
Who touch'd a jarring lyre at first,
But ever strove to make it true:

Perplext in faith, but pure in deeds,
At last he beat his music out.
There lives more faith in honest doubt,
Believe me, than in half the creeds.

He fought his doubts and gather'd strength,
He would not make his judgment blind,
He faced the spectres of the mind
And laid them: thus he came at length

To find a stronger faith his own;
And Power was with him in the night,
Which makes the darkness and the light,
And dwells not in the light alone,

But in the darkness and the cloud,
As over Sinai's peaks of old,
While Israel made their gods of gold,
Altho' the trumpet blew so loud.

We turn in the last two days of this week to the other poet for whom doubt and self-questioning opened up a path to deeper truth and renewed faith. It is this conviction that God might in fact be nearer to us when we doubt and struggle than when we bask in certainty that informs the extraordinary courage and honesty of Tennyson's great poem *In Memoriam*. Although written over many years, this poem was occasioned by the death of Tennyson's closest friend, Arthur Henry Hallam, the man with whom he had shared his great love of poetry, his personal sorrows and joys, and above all his conviction that personal honesty combined with free and open enquiry were the only ways to establish truth and personal conviction. The whole poem is a kind of spiritual journal, a series of intimate lyrics taking the poet from the first extremities of grief, through radical doubt that there is any goodness in the world, and finally towards a renewed and profound faith in the God who is Love. Today and tomorrow we read two extracts from this extraordinary poem.

Towards the end of *In Memoriam* Tennyson addresses those who condemn doubters as weak while suppressing or demonizing their own doubts. He shows instead that a mature and balanced faith is not one that has refused the agony and the wrestling but one that has been through them and grown from the experience. Paradoxically, in this famous passage about 'faith in honest doubt' he also makes one of his most explicit appeals to scripture, to the darkness and cloud of Sinai, contrasted with the sparkling certainties of the Golden Calf.

There is an interesting personal note to add to today's extract. The first line, 'You tell me, doubt is Devil-born', may well have been addressed to Emily Selwood, the brilliant woman who would become Tennyson's wife and without whom, it is fair to say, a great deal of his poetry would never have been written. In the crisis that followed Hallam's death Tennyson entered a protracted period of doubt and depression. His brooding melancholy seemed perhaps to confirm the rumours of the supposed Tennyson 'bad blood', for he came from a family prone to mental breakdown. Tennyson's father was a violent alcoholic who drank himself to death and some of his brothers exhibited similar behaviour. Further, in giving voice to his doubts Tennyson found himself accused of atheism. Emily, who loved him, was forbidden to see him or correspond with him; as a devout Christian she was anxious about whether she could or should marry a man whose faith, at that time, seemed so weak. But as he brought his great poem to its conclusion he arranged for someone to send it to Emily, and when she read it she realized that Tennyson was indeed the right man for her. They were married in 1850, the year of its publication and the year he was made Poet Laureate. An *annus mirabilis* indeed.

SATURDAY

Strong Son of God, Immortal Love *Alfred Tennyson*

Strong Son of God, immortal Love,
Whom we, that have not seen thy face,
By faith, and faith alone, embrace,
Believing where we cannot prove;

...

Our little systems have their day;
They have their day and cease to be:
They are but broken lights of thee,
And thou, O Lord, art more than they.

We have but faith: we cannot know;
For knowledge is of things we see;
And yet we trust it comes from thee,
A beam in darkness: let it grow.

Let knowledge grow from more to more,
But more of reverence in us dwell;
That mind and soul, according well,
May make one music as before ...

This prayer is placed at the opening of *In Memoriam*. Though it
appears at the beginning of his poem, Tennyson could not have
written it until he had been through the journey of grieving and
expressed so much of the doubt and bitterness that necessarily
preceded this final act of trust; so it was, perhaps, the last part
that he wrote.

Though he was born in a vicarage (or perhaps because he was born in a vicarage!) Tennyson had great struggles with faith; like many young students before and since, he had all but abandoned his faith by the time he came up to university. Home life had been horrible and at Cambridge he made great friendships that he hoped would last a lifetime. With his new friends he freely explored the new science, the optimism of the nineteenth century, and the fresh horizons opening up on every side. And then the closest of his friends, Arthur Hallam, died. In the shock of grief Tennyson began to fear that what the 'new science' revealed was not a caring God or a purposeful world but a 'nature' whose processes were grim and mindless, a cosmos indifferent to suffering. It is from *In Memoriam* that we get the phrase 'nature red in tooth and claw', and even before Darwin had published his theories Tennyson looked to the fossil record and heard from nature only the voice of indifference:

From scarped cliff and quarried stone
She cries, 'A thousand types are gone:
I care for nothing, all shall go.'

And yet, as we saw in yesterday's extract, he never ceased to seek for a faith that could live with and through doubt and grief. The poem spans the whole range of our emotions from the times when we are just 'an infant crying in the night: an infant crying for the light: and with no language but a cry', to moments when we are aware of sudden glimpses of order, the surges of hope that call us to 'ring out the grief that saps the mind ... ring in redress for all mankind'.

And so at the end of his long exploration of doubt and faith, despair and hope, Tennyson makes this prayer. An act of trust in the God who is Love, it is very much a prayer for our time. In an age when increasingly strident forms of scientific and religious fundamentalism are making absolute truth-claims over against one another we need to make this prayer our own.

A key verse in this extract carries the insight that:

Our little systems have their day;
They have their day and cease to be:
They are but broken lights of thee,
And thou, O Lord, art more than they.

To pray this prayer is to acknowledge the limits of knowledge,
to know just how little our 'little systems' are. It is to ask for the
grace and humility to trust: to trust God and one another. And
yet from out of that humility this prayer asks for the wisdom
to cherish real advances in knowledge, to see the discoveries of
science as a partner to the discoveries of faith, to see 'mind and
soul according well', making 'one music'.

Prayer that Pierces:
The Point of the Passion

PASSION SUNDAY

The Incarnate One *Edwin Muir*

The windless northern surge, the sea-gull's scream,
And Calvin's kirk crowning the barren brae.
I think of Giotto the Tuscan shepherd's dream,
Christ, man and creature in their inner day.
How could our race betray
The Image, and the Incarnate One unmake
Who chose this form and fashion for our sake?

The Word made flesh here is made word again
A word made word in flourish and arrogant crook.
See there King Calvin with his iron pen,
And God three angry letters in a book,
And there the logical hook
On which the Mystery is impaled and bent
Into an ideological argument.

There's better gospel in man's natural tongue,
And truer sight was theirs outside the Law
Who saw the far side of the Cross among
The archaic peoples in their ancient awe,
In ignorant wonder saw
The wooden cross-tree on the bare hillside,
Not knowing that there a God suffered and died.

The fleshless word, growing, will bring us down,
Pagan and Christian man alike will fall,
The auguries say, the white and black and brown,
The merry and the sad, theorist, lover, all
Invisibly will fall:
Abstract calamity, save for those who can
Build their cold empire on the abstract man.

A soft breeze stirs and all my thoughts are blown
Far out to sea and lost. Yet I know well
The bloodless word will battle for its own
Invisibly in brain and nerve and cell.
The generations tell
Their personal tale: the One has far to go
Past the mirages and the murdering snow.

We come to Passion Sunday, and in this final week we look to
the cross to find in it, as Paul suggests, both 'the power of God
and the Wisdom of God'. But the problem is, how do we look?
Edwin Muir's powerful poem 'The Incarnate One' warns us
against the dangers of theological abstraction and urges us to try
and stay with the Incarnation, with flesh and blood, to drop our
'ideological argument' and look again at the cross in 'ignorant
wonder'.

This is a prophetic poem that calls us to realize that, ironically,
it is the Christian Church itself that has refused the true meaning
of the Incarnation, and so, beyond it, of the cross. We have been
trying, he says, to 'unmake' the Incarnate One, to refuse the gift
of God's solidarity with us in our flesh, his closeness, and instead
push him back to some infinite distance of abstraction. In so doing
we 'betray the image', we prefer 'the bloodless word', the 'cold
empire' of the 'abstract man'. In a chilling and utterly memorable
line Muir sums up the way the abstract theology of 'Calvin's Kirk',
the Scottish church of his boyhood, had substituted its syllogisms
for the incarnate, image-laden, flesh and blood presence of Christ:
'The Word made flesh here is made word again'. Indeed he goes
on to describe this unmaking of the Incarnation, this turning God

into syllogism and proposition in terms that frame it as a further crucifixion:

> And there the logical hook
> On which the Mystery is impaled and bent
> Into an ideological argument.

The miracle of the poem is that Muir is able to use words, language, the very medium that he felt was discarnating Christ, as a means of appeal, as a way of rooting us back into the Incarnate One 'who chose this form and fashion for our sake'. Although he is wary of any God who is just 'three angry letters in a book', he is also aware that there is indeed gospel in 'man's natural tongue'. He takes us, in a daring image, to see

> the far side of the Cross among
> The archaic peoples in their ancient awe,

suggesting that we must learn to look again at 'the wooden cross-tree on the bare hillside' in 'ignorant wonder', forgetting for a moment our neatly packaged theologies of atonement, for a moment 'not knowing that there a God suffered and died', so that we can begin again with the visceral reality of the cross itself.

Then comes an extraordinary turn at the end of the poem. Muir foresees how the flight into abstraction, particularly theological abstraction, might dehumanize us, and almost undo our own incarnation:

> The fleshless word, growing, will bring us down,
> Pagan and Christian man alike will fall ...
> Abstract calamity, save for those who can
> Build their cold empire on the abstract man.

But then, at the very end of the poem, even as he foresees the ways in which

> The bloodless word will battle for its own
> Invisibly in brain and nerve and cell

he suddenly brings us back to Christ, the Incarnate One of the poem's title, and suggests that perhaps the Incarnation itself is not yet complete, and will not be until it is complete in us; 'the One has far to go'. It may be that the way to defeat the 'abstract calamity', to get past what he calls 'the mirages and the murdering snow', is for 'the generations' to 'tell their personal tale': for each generation to find for itself again the truly incarnate Christ, grasping that gospel in their natural tongue. Certainly this poem helps us to do just that.

MONDAY

Golgotha *John Heath-Stubbs*

In the middle of the world, in the centre
Of the polluted heart of man, a midden;
A stake stemmed in the rubbish.

From lipless jaws, Adam's skull
Gasped up through the garbage:
'I lie in the discarded dross of history,
Ground down again to the red dust,
The obliterated image. Create me.'

From lips cracked with thirst, the voice
That sounded once over the billows of chaos
When the royal banners advanced,
replied through the smother of dark:
'All is accomplished, all is made new, and look –
All things, once more, are good.'

Then, with a loud cry, exhaled His spirit.

One key to the mystery of the Gospels is the truth that everything
that happened 'out there and back then' also happens 'in here and
right now'. Christ is the second Adam, the second human being in
whom we are all gathered up. What he does *for* us, he also does *in*
us. Just as hidden in us somewhere is the Eden we once inhabited
and have lost, so also somewhere in us is Golgotha. John Heath-
Stubbs meditates on this as he imagines at 'the place of the skull'

the Old Adam's skull speaking to the New Adam and making a prayer for all of us. The poem ends with the astonishing paradox that the death of Christ is the beginning of a new creation, a breathing out of the Spirit to make all things new.

So, like Dante's *Commedia*, this poem starts 'in the middle':

> In the middle of the world, in the centre
> Of the polluted heart of man, a midden;
> A stake stemmed in the rubbish.

The word 'midden' may come as a shock, but it reminds us that Golgotha was indeed a rubbish heap, a place where the unclean offscourings of Jerusalem were thrown. That is why the Romans chose to crucify Jews there; they knew that the particular veneration in Judaism for the clean and the holy would make death in such an unclean place peculiarly horrific. But that is also why our Lord chose to die there. 'He was made to be sin, who knew no sin, that we might become the righteousness of God.' He identifies with us, not in our carefully presented surfaces, but in our 'polluted heart'. In these lines Heath-Stubbs may be recalling Yeats' brilliant lines at the end of 'The Circus Animals' Desertion':

> I must lie down where all the ladders start
> In the foul rag-and-bone shop of the heart.

But this 'middle of the world', this 'centre of the polluted heart of man', is the scene not only of crucifixion but of new creation. The discarded skull, frequently seen in paintings of the crucifixion, becomes the voice of Adam, of all fallen humanity, appealing to Christ from the 'red earth' from which Adam was taken and named, but also gasping up 'through the garbage', through the detritus of his own sin. 'Create me'! Your image in me has been 'obliterated', Adam is saying; but you, crucified with and for me on this rubbish dump, can make me new again.

And then comes the wonderful turn at the end of the poem. Without in any way veiling or minimizing the sheer human agony of the cross – the 'lips cracked with thirst' – Heath-Stubbs summons the full resonance of the first creation: the Word of God creating all things, the Spirit moving over the face of the deep, bringing order to 'the billows of chaos'. Christ's final words, 'It is finished!', become not an end but a beginning, the making of a new creation. The 'last breath' in which he 'exhaled His spirit' becomes also the moment of new creation:

'All is accomplished, all is made new, and look –
All things, once more, are good.'

TUESDAY

The Agony *George Herbert*

Philosophers have measur'd mountains,
  Fathom'd the depths of seas, of states and kings;
  Walk'd with a staff to heav'n and traced fountains:
    But there are two vast, spacious thins,
  The which to measure it doth more behove;
  Yet few there are that sound them, – Sin and Love.

  Who would know Sin, let him repair
Unto Mount Olivet; there shall he see
A Man so wrung with pains, that all His hair,
    His skin, His garments bloody be.
Sin is that press and vice, which forceth pain
To hunt his cruel food through ev'ry vein.

  Who knows not Love, let him assay
And taste that juice which, on the cross, a pike
Did set again abroach; then let him say
    If ever he did taste the like,
Love is that liquor sweet and most divine,
Which my God feels as blood, but I as wine.

In 'Golgotha' we looked with John Heath-Stubbs at how the whole of humanity is involved in the Passion, understood as both death and renewal. In 'The Agony' by George Herbert we see how the Passion of Christ, from his agony in the garden to the shedding of his blood on the cross, helps us entirely to reconfigure and renew our understanding first of sin and then of the love that meets and redeems it.

The first three lines of this poem sum up our apparently impressive but actually empty ways of knowing. From there Herbert turns to deal with what is missing from the empty heart of such merely outer knowledge:

> The which to measure it doth more behove;
> Yet few there are that sound them, – Sin and Love.

'Sin and Love'. How are we to know these things? Our own age would make the knowledge purely personal and self-contained – a little dip into what we think we know about our private psychology. Herbert has a quite different approach. Our only hope of real self-knowledge is to look for a light beyond ourselves and come to know God, who knows us better than we can know ourselves, so that one day we can 'know even as we have been fully known' (1 Corinthians 13.12). For Herbert, the only way we can know God, the only possible place and person in which we can meet him is Christ. In Christ God meets us in our humanity. It is from the Passion of Christ that we learn both who God is and who we are. In the vivid images of the second stanza of this poem Herbert is saying that Christ's agony in the garden is also an image of our inner condition: an image both of what Sin does to a person and also of God's loving response, which bears and transforms the sheer weight of sin. The very fact that Jesus had to endure such agony in order to deliver us from 'that press and vice' reveals how serious a thing sin is.

The image of Christ crushed in the 'press and vice' is profound; it not only expresses the pain and pressure of Gethsemane, squeezing the very blood to the surface of Christ's body, it also alludes to the rich biblical symbolism of the winepress. The winepress symbolizes both wrath and generosity. Isaiah describes the winepress of wrath: 'I have trodden the winepress alone ... for I will treat them in mine anger, and trample them in my fury; and their blood shall be sprinkled upon my garments, and I will stain all my raiment' (Isaiah 63.3, AV). But this image of a wrathful God, coming covered in the blood of those upon whom he has taken just vengeance, was daringly and paradoxically applied to Christ by the Church Fathers, suggesting that in making atonement it is his own blood that Christ spills instead of ours, and also making a symbolically profound reversal of the Old Testament metaphor. In Isaiah the juice from the crushed grapes symbolizes blood. In the radical Christian reading of that passage the garments dipped in blood presage Christ's gift of his own blood as wine. And all this symbolic background is focused, and *expressed* (in every sense of that term), in the concentrated imagery of the poem; the sign of wrath becomes the sign of redemption as 'Sin' is transmuted by 'Love' and from this 'press' flows the wine that will be the life of the communicant Church. So in his third and final stanza Herbert moves from the contemplation in Christ of 'Sin' to contemplation in Christ of that 'Love' that redeems sin. He who trod the wine-press alone becomes the cask of wine to be pierced, 'set again abroach', opened to refresh his people. It is an astonishing and daring metaphor to make the moment the soldier's pike pierces Christ's heart on the cross a vision of the opening of a wine cask:

Who knows not Love, let him assay
And taste that juice which, on the cross, a pike
Did set again abroach;

The poem finishes with an expression of the mystery of Incarnation and sacrament which is God's divine exchange and intercommunion offered to man on the cross:

Love is that liquor sweet and most divine,
Which my God feels as blood, but I as wine.

WEDNESDAY

Gethsemane *Rowan Williams*

Who said that trees grow easily
compared with us? What if the bright
bare load that pushes down on them
insisted that they spread and bowed
and pleated back on themselves and cracked
and hunched? Light dropping like a palm
levelling the ground, backwards and forwards?

Across the valley are the other witnesses
of two millennia, the broad stones
packed by the hand of God, bristling
with little messages to fill the cracks.
As the light falls and flattens what grows
on these hills, the fault lines dart and spread,
there is room to say something, quick and tight.

Into the trees' clefts, then, do we push
our folded words, thick as thumbs?
Somewhere inside the ancient bark, a voice
has been before us, pushed the densest word
of all, abba, and left it to be collected by
whoever happens to be passing, bent down
the same way by the hot unreadable palms.

Like the second verse of 'The Agony', this poem is set in Geth-semane. Rowan Williams may well have had Herbert's image of the 'press and vice' in his mind; he is certainly aware that the place-name Gethsemane in the Greek New Testament is derived from the Aramaic word *gat-smane*, meaning 'oil press', for Gethsemane is an olive grove that would have contained an olive press. He is aware too that some of the ancient olive trees in Gethsemane today are 2,000 years old and may well have been witness to Christ's agony. And it is that realization, that sense both of the continuity of witness and also of crisis, that gives this poem its presence and energy.

We start with a sense of the intense brightness of the sun experienced as a 'bright bare load' pushing down on the trees themselves, something that is suggested by the very shape of these ancient trees:

> spread and bowed
> and pleated back on themselves and cracked
> and hunched?

Williams asks imagination's favourite question, 'What if?' What if these ancient trees express the way we ourselves deal with pres-sure – both the pressures of life in crisis and the insistent pressure of the Divine? Then the scene shifts across the valley, from the sacred Christian site to the sacred Jewish one, the Western Wall:

> Across the valley are the other witnesses
> of two millennia, the broad stones
> packed by the hand of God, bristling
> with little messages to fill the cracks.

There too the insistent heat and light is felt like a tight-packing pressure. Is it God who puts on the pressure or God who feels it? Surely the answer in this similarly densely packed and ambivalent poem is 'both'! For now we switch back from the Wailing Wall to Gethsemane and find ourselves praying there, under pressure, with Christ. Just as the prayers of the devout have been pressed as 'little messages' into the cracks of the Western Wall, so we have a moment of possibility, 'room to say something, quick and tight', to 'push our folded words' into the clefts of an ancient olive tree that was there when Christ prayed in that garden under the intense pressure of the divine Agony. And so the poem turns, coming suddenly upon its heart and meaning, finding Christ's own prayer, still being uttered deep within the tree:

> somewhere inside the ancient bark, a voice
> has been before us, pushed the densest word
> of all, abba,

And 'abba', that 'densest word of all', packed intensely in that agony with both Christ's love for his Father and his sense of abandonment, is also the word that truly links the two scenes of the poem – the Wailing Wall, witness of two millennia of exile and abandonment, and the Garden of Gethsemane, witness of the God who entered into and experienced that abandonment with humanity. And the olive tree itself, the witness and symbol of peace in a deeply conflicted region, is also, in Paul's letter to the Romans, the symbol of how Judaism and Christianity, with their 'witness of millennia' to the One God, share common roots and may at last be grafted back into one another.

THURSDAY

I wake and feel the fell of dark *G. M. Hopkins*

I wake and feel the fell of dark, not day,
What hours, O what black hours we have spent
This night! what sights you, heart, saw; ways you went!
And more must, in yet longer light's delay.
With witness I speak this. But where I say
Hours I mean years, mean life. And my lament
Is cries countless, cries like dead letters sent
To dearest him that lives alas! away.

I am gall, I am heartburn. God's most deep decree
Bitter would have me taste: my taste was me;
Bones built in me, flesh filled, blood brimmed the curse.
Selfyeast of spirit a dull dough sours. I see
The lost are like this, and their scourge to be
As I am mine, their sweating selves; but worse.

We continue to explore this idea of the press and pressure of
Gethsemane in two sonnets by Gerard Manley Hopkins. Today's
poem is one of a set of sonnets sometimes known as the 'terrible'
sonnets, not because they are in the modern sense 'terrible' poetry,
but because, as Hopkins' friend Canon Dixon said, they reached
the 'terrible crystal'. That is to say, they expressed in perfect
form the human experience of terror and darkness. But there is a
paradox here. Anyone who has experienced, as Hopkins clearly
did, that 'fell of dark' which is profound depression, will know
that part of the agony of that experience, of hanging, as he put

it in another poem, on the mind's 'cliffs of fall, sheer, frightful, no-man-fathomed', is the sheer isolation of grief, the feeling that we are alone in our pain, and that no one else can possibly have experienced this or could possibly understand it. So when someone, especially a poet of this calibre, has the courage to put this into words, there is, for the person who has suffered like this, an experience not only of recognition but also of relief, and release: 'At last someone has said it, at last I can put words to what I went through! And even if in one way it takes me back to the experience, in another way it sets me free, and gives me a handle to deal with it.'

But when we read Hopkins' 'terrible' sonnets, something else comes into play. Hopkins was a man of great faith, in profound communion with Christ. His courage and honesty in expressing this experience of darkness gives the lie to the pernicious idea that faith is an instant salve and Christians ought to be cheerful all the time; it also allows the Christian who experiences depression a sense of solidarity, not only with other Christians who have experienced the same thing, but with Christ himself, even, and especially, if at the time of the depression itself they have no conscious sense of his presence. Paradoxically God is palpably present, often as a hidden interlocutor, in the very poems that are cries of agony at his absence. For this is the paradox at the heart of Christ's own cry of dereliction from the cross: 'My God, my God, why have you forsaken me?' Even at the moment of dereliction Christ is still addressing his father, and that is why, in 'Gethsemane', Rowan Williams describes 'abba' as 'the densest word of all'. Indeed, today's poem is in its own way, like the previous two and the one we will read tomorrow, a reflection on Gethsemane and the agony in the garden.

This poem is surely for anyone who has woken to bitterness and misery in the small hours, enduring the long wait for 'yet longer light's delay', a dawn that never seems to come. It is a poem for those who feel that all their prayers have become, as it were, 'dead letters', messages sent to someone who is not replying, who 'lives alas! away'. And yet the whole poem is somehow written and confessed in God's presence, searching 'God's most deep decree'.

The dead letters are still there, waiting to be collected, waiting for a resurrection. Indeed I think Rowan Williams was recalling and in some sense answering this poem by Hopkins; he uses the same message/letter image to describe Christ's own prayer to his father in Gethsemane:

> a voice
> has been before us, pushed the densest word
> of all, abba, and left it to be collected

But it is the very last sentence of the Hopkins poem, the seemingly unredeemed ending, that establishes the deepest implicit link with Gethsemane:

> I see
> The lost are like this, and their scourge to be
> As I am mine, their sweating selves; but worse.

Here, just as Hopkins counts himself as one of 'the lost', he evokes the agony and bloody sweat of Christ in Gethsemane. And that is the point. In that agony Christ identified himself utterly and for ever with the lost, so that, utterly and for ever, they might be found.

FRIDAY

God's Grandeur *G. M. Hopkins*

The world is charged with the grandeur of God.
It will flame out, like shining from shook foil;
It gathers to a greatness, like the ooze of oil
Crushed. Why do men then now not reck his rod?
Generations have trod, have trod, have trod;
And all is seared with trade; bleared, smeared with toil;
And wears man's smudge and shares man's smell: the soil
Is bare now, nor can foot feel, being shod.

And for all this, nature is never spent;
There lives the dearest freshness deep down things;
And though the last lights off the black West went
Oh, morning, at the brown brink eastward, springs –
Because the Holy Ghost over the bent
World broods with warm breast and with ah! bright wings.

And now, coming up for air, feeling our way into the light, we
come to one of Hopkins' most beautiful, most hopeful, most cele-
brated poems. And what, you may well ask, has it to do with
Passiontide's dark journey? Surely this poem belongs with R. S.
Thomas' 'Bright Field', and Heaney's 'Postscript', those poems
that celebrate how, as Elizabeth Barrett Browning said in *Aurora
Leigh,*

Earth's crammed with heaven,
And every common bush afire with God;

And it is true, that is indeed what this poem is about. It celebrates, as Coleridge said poetry should, 'the dearest freshness deep down things', and deeper still, the glory and grandeur of God himself, charged like a great and hidden power into the very core of his world, ready at any moment to 'flame out, like shining from shook foil'.

But look a little closer. How is the world 'charged' with this grandeur? What makes it flame out? First notice the triple sense of the word 'charged'. First it is 'charged' in the sense of filled full, packed down and filled again, like the powerful charge of gunpowder in a musket; from that comes the sense of a live 'charge', a charge of electricity, of a hidden element that carries 'a charge' ready to leap out and across at a moment of contact with another conducting element. But is there not also another sense that the world is charged with the grandeur of God – charged with a task, with a challenge? The gospel is a 'charge' in all these senses. 'A charge to keep I have' we sing in the hymn, and the gospel itself is powerful and explosive. At any moment it can and does flame out in people's lives, in entire communities, illuminating the world like lightning, as Jesus said he would: 'For as the lightning comes from the east and flashes as far as the west, so will be the coming of the Son of Man' (Matthew 24.27).

And what makes it flame out, what releases the charge into the world? How does the grandeur, the greatness of God gather and become apparent?

It gathers to a greatness, like the ooze of oil
Crushed.

'Crushed' is the key word in this poem, and it is the link with Gethsemane. Gethsemane, you remember, means 'oil press'. It is in the press and pressure of Gethsemane that God's grandeur 'gathers to a greatness'. There, where we least expect it, that deepest charge of glory is to be found. This is also the heart of John's Gospel. The constant question in the first part of that Gospel is when and how God's glory is going to be revealed: when is the 'hour' coming? And when it comes, it is not at the brightest moment but at the darkest. It happens in the transition between John 13.30 and 31, just as Judas goes out to betray him and begin the chain of events that will lead to Gethsemane and the cross:

> So, after receiving the piece of bread, he immediately went out. And it was night.
>
> When he had gone out, Jesus said, 'Now the Son of Man has been glorified, and God has been glorified in him. God will also glorify him in himself and will glorify him at once.'

Christ has come to be crushed, crushed with us, so that in him, through him, and for us, the glory might be revealed and the oil pressed. The oil that is his *eleison*, his mercy and healing, poured into the world.

SATURDAY

Love's as warm as tears *C. S. Lewis*

Love's as warm as tears,
   Love is tears:
Pressure within the brain,
Tension at the throat,
Deluge, weeks of rain,
Haystacks afloat,
Featureless seas between
Hedges, where once was green.

Love's as fierce as fire,
   Love is fire:
All sorts – Infernal heat
Clinkered with greed and pride,
Lyric desire, sharp-sweet,
Laughing, even when denied,
And that empyreal flame
Whence all loves came.

Love's as fresh as spring,
   Love is spring:
Bird-song in the air,
Cool smells in a wood,
Whispering 'Dare! Dare!'
To sap, to blood,
Telling 'Ease, safety, rest,
Are good; not best.'

Love's as hard as nails,
   Love is nails:
Blunt, thick, hammered through
The medial nerves of One
Who, having made us, knew
The thing He had done,
Seeing (with all that is)
Our cross, and His.

Someone who knew both doubt and faith, and whose own journey through and from atheism made him an all the more effective Christian apologist, was C. S. Lewis. Famous as a theologian and a children's writer, he is less well known as a poet, but wrote some very fine verse. The poem 'Love's as warm as tears' seems to go to the heart of both our human loving and the divine and costly love revealed to us on the cross. Lewis, a medieval scholar, has subtly woven the four elements, and perhaps more faintly the four seasons, into these meditative verses on Love. So we begin with water, with love 'as warm as tears', moving from the first inner 'tension at the throat', preceding long held-back tears, to the outer image of the floods that come at last:

Deluge, weeks of rain,
Haystacks afloat,
Featureless seas between
Hedges, where once was green.

Then we turn to the second element of fire; just as Dante at the end of the 'Purgatorio' was aware of how the same flame could represent our very different loves – human and divine – so Lewis deftly touches on the different senses in which Love is fire, finishing with the fire of Divine Love:

that empyreal flame
Whence all loves came.

Then we meet the element of air, evoked in the 'spring' verse:

Bird-song in the air,
Cool smells in a wood ...

And finally we come to 'earth', the last and lowest, the hardest of
the elements. And here Lewis' lyric achieves one of the things that
poetry does best, which is to take a cliché, which is 'dead language
that won't lie down', wake it up, and breathe new life in it. So
Lewis takes the cliché 'hard as nails' and turns it into a key with
which to open up the Passion:

> Love's as hard as nails,
>   Love is nails:
> Blunt, thick, hammered through
> The medial nerves of One
> Who, having made us, knew
> The thing He had done,
> Seeing (with all that is)
> Our cross, and His.

The short, sharp sounds of 'blunt, thick, hammered' and the
wrenching medical accuracy of 'medial nerves' serve to keep the
crucifixion visceral and incarnate, and yet through that Lewis
moves to a profound theology of both creation and atonement,
simply and beautifully expressed. From the beginning of Creation
God had foreseen the sorrow our misused freedom might bring,
and chosen, from the beginning and in that knowledge, to share
with us the consequences of our own mistakes, that he might
redeem us from them.

WEEK 6

Palm Sunday and Holy Week

PALM SUNDAY

Palm Sunday *Malcolm Guite*

Now to the gate of my Jerusalem,
The seething holy city of my heart,
The Saviour comes. But will I welcome him?
Oh crowds of easy feelings make a start;
They raise their hands, get caught up in the singing,
And think the battle won. Too soon they'll find
The challenge, the reversal he is bringing
Changes their tune. I know what lies behind
The surface flourish that so quickly fades;
Self-interest, and fearful guardedness,
The hardness of the heart, its barricades,
And at the core, the dreadful emptiness
Of a perverted temple. Jesus, come
Break my resistance and make me your home.

Holy Week is perhaps its own season, distinct from Lent, the week
for which Lent is preparing us and towards which it is pointing.
So we have come to the end and edge of our wilderness journey,
out beyond Jordan and back again, and now we find ourselves
standing with another crowd of pilgrims, all preparing, on Palm
Sunday, to enter Jerusalem. Between now and Maundy Thursday
I share a sequence of sonnets for Holy Week from my collection
Sounding the Seasons. In composing these sonnets I had in mind
that mysterious and beautiful phrase in the Psalms about the man
'in whose heart are the highways to Zion' (Psalm 84.5). I wanted
to develop the hint offered in that phrase that there is an inner

as well as an outer Jerusalem, and that therefore the events of
Holy Week are both about Jesus' outward, visible and historical
entry into Jerusalem and what he did there and then, and also
about his entry into the inner Jerusalem, the 'seething holy city'
as I have called it, of our own hearts. I wanted to explore what it
might mean to say that we have our own gates, walls and watch-
towers, that somewhere within us there is both a temple and a
seat of judgement, and both might need to be challenged and
cleansed. And I wanted to imagine that within us there is a 'house
at Bethany', space for a more intimate encounter with Jesus, for
healing, anointing and blessing.

So in today's poem I let the outer story of Palm Sunday pose
some questions for my inner life. What would it really mean to
welcome Jesus as King into the Zion of one's own heart? How is
the city already occupied and governed? Who is in charge now
and how is power divided? Is there an uneasy compromise in my
own inner Jerusalem, such as there was in the outer Jerusalem of
Jesus' time? Is there a grand-looking temple where lots of time-
worn rituals can be repeated as long as it makes no trouble for
the secular administration? And that secular administration – the
bit of me that makes the day-to-day financial decisions, about
who should have my time, for how long and for how much, the
administration that decides what to buy and what to sell, what
to acquire and what to lose – for whom is it really working? Am
I in charge there? Or is my governing ego, like Pontius Pilate,
really and fearfully beholden to another power structure? Are the
big corporations and their advertisers actually running the show,
manipulating my sense of what I need? Perhaps the Pilate of our
little ego is in fact working for their empire. And what about
the general population of my heart? The crowds of feelings and
memories and thoughts, caught between the temple and the court,
swaying this way and that, are not sure who to follow, or where
their true loyalty lies. Can I invite Jesus in to all of that? And if I
do, what will happen?

MONDAY

Jesus weeps *Malcolm Guite*

Jesus comes near and he beholds the city
And looks on us with tears in his eyes,
And wells of mercy, streams of love and pity
Flow from the fountain whence all things arise.
He loved us into life and longs to gather
And meet with his beloved face to face.
How often has he called, a careful mother,
And wept for our refusals of his grace,
Wept for a world that, weary with its weeping,
Benumbed and stumbling, turns the other way;
Fatigued compassion is already sleeping
Whilst her worst nightmares stalk the light of day.
But we might waken yet, and face those fears,
If we could see ourselves through Jesus' tears.

Today's sonnet is a meditation on a single verse in Luke's Gospel,
chapter 19 verse 41: 'As he came near and saw the city, he wept
over it.' It's hard to see through tears, but sometimes it's the only
way to see. Tears can be the turning point, the springs of renewal;
to know you have been wept for is to know that you are loved.

I have a God who knows what it is to weep and who weeps for
me, weeps with me, understands to the depths and from the inside
the *rerum lachrymae*, the tears of things.

So the octet of this sonnet (its first eight lines) contemplates
the tears of Christ, his infinite compassion; but when the 'turn',
the 'volta', comes in line 9, I turn to think about our own 'weep-

ing', about the sources and limits of our own compassion. And here I confront that extraordinary and telling modern phrase 'compassion fatigue'. Our capacity for compassion, literally to be *com* with or alongside the *passio*, the suffering, of others, is God-given and is part of his image in us. It is natural and right that when we feel compassion we should have the desire to act, to do something to respond to and alleviate the suffering we witness. And for most of human history most human beings experiencing compassion would have had the chance to do something immediate and particular about it because any suffering they witnessed would be local to them; they could at least begin to engage in the great 'works of mercy' of which Jesus speaks in Matthew, to feed the hungry, to clothe the naked, to visit the sick. But because of instant news exchange, our generation has the daily experience of exposure to suffering on a large scale that is at once vivid and distant. We see the hungry, the naked and the ill every evening on our TV screens but we cannot immediately or directly contact the person whose tears we are seeing, whose tears may have provoked our own.

What to do? Of course we can support the relevant NGOs, we can contribute to the DEC appeal, and we know, intellectually, that we are making a difference, however small. But still we are haunted by that particular face, the one whose actual need we saw, whose desperate need we couldn't meet. The danger then is that the natural link between compassion and action is severed; compassion freewheels in its own frustration and burns out. We can't deal with it any more and so the world, 'weary with its weeping, benumbed and stumbling, turns the other way'.

Then, if we are not careful, compassion fatigue becomes a long sleep or even the death of our capacity for fellow feeling:

Fatigued compassion is already sleeping
Whilst her worst nightmares stalk the light of day.

Again, what can we do? Jesus comes close to us, and this is where we particularly need to come close to him, for his compassion, unlike ours, is infinite. Ours can be renewed in his, our compassion not just for the world but for ourselves. We need first to receive and feel his healing compassion for us, in our very state of compassion fatigue; in so doing the healing springs can rise again and our own capacity for compassion will be renewed.

TUESDAY

Cleansing the Temple *Malcolm Guite*

Come to your Temple here with liberation
And overturn these tables of exchange,
Restore in me my lost imagination,
Begin in me for good the pure change.
Come as you came, an infant with your mother,
That innocence may cleanse and claim this ground.
Come as you came, a boy who sought his father
With questions asked and certain answers found.
Come as you came this day, a man in anger,
Unleash the lash that drives a pathway through,
Face down for me the fear, the shame, the danger,
Teach me again to whom my love is due.
Break down in me the barricades of death
And tear the veil in two with your last breath.

When Solomon dedicated the temple he rightly declared that not even the heaven of heavens could contain almighty God, much less this temple made with hands; yet God himself still came into the temple. He came as a baby, the essence of all light and purity in human flesh; he came as a young boy full of questions, seeking to know his father's will; and today he came in righteous anger to clear away the blasphemous barriers that human power-games try to throw up between God and the world he loves. Finally, by his death on the cross he took away the last barrier in the temple, and in our hearts, the veil that stood between us and the holy of holies, the very presence of God, in us and beyond us.

This sonnet reflects on all four of those advents of God to the temple, but focuses on his advent to the inner temple of the heart, on the challenge and cleansing that must happen there. On this day Jesus 'overturned the tables of exchange'. It's very clear what that might mean for both the outward and visible Church and for the world at large. It represents a challenge to the dominance of finance, to the deification of the market. It is a call to take down the financial barriers that prevent people and whole nations from developing fully as they should. But what might the tables of exchange be in our inner temple? In the outer temple one kind of currency was being exchanged for another, one set of terms for another. And that is happening in us all the time, as we change terms between the outer and the inner, between the language of the world and the language of our hearts. There is a right and proper way to do this that is rich and imaginative, but there is also a cold and calculating way, a temptation to cash everything out as a payment to the ego. We need the exchange to work two ways; we need to be able to take the little tokens of our own feelings and imaginatively exchange them for a real understanding of the feelings of others. That is why today's sonnet begins with a petition to Christ:

Come to your Temple here with liberation
And overturn these tables of exchange,
Restore in me my lost imagination,
Begin in me for good the pure change.

Then I ask for Christ to come in all his ways: as the infant to claim and renew my infancy, and all that is and should remain child-like in me; as a questioning boy, that I too might have the courage to question the learned doctors of the Church and offer some insights too; as a man of zeal and passion, that he might stir in me a proper anger and courage in the face of injustice. But it is the last of his comings to the temple that changes everything, and for that we will have to wait for Good Friday, though we anticipate it a little here. For that final visit to the temple is done, paradoxically, from the cross, when as Jesus breathes his last the veil in the temple is torn in two from top to bottom. As Hebrews tells us, that veil hangs between heaven and earth, and Christ, the great high priest, has gone within the veil on our behalf and brings not just our outer names but our inner nature into the heart of heaven itself – the heaven of which the temple, both outward and inner, was only a type and shadow.

WEDNESDAY

The Anointing at Bethany *Malcolm Guite*

Come close with Mary, Martha, Lazarus,
So close the candles flare with their soft breath,
And kindle heart and soul to flame within us
Lit by these mysteries of life and death.
For beauty now begins the final movement,
In quietness and intimate encounter,
The alabaster jar of precious ointment
Is broken open for the world's true lover.
The whole room richly fills to feast the senses
With all the yearning such a fragrance brings,
The heart is mourning but the spirit dances,
Here at the very centre of all things,
Here at the meeting place of love and loss
We all foresee and see beyond the cross.

John 12.1–8 tells us of how Mary of Bethany anointed Jesus. I love this intense and beautiful moment in the Gospel. The God of the cosmos enters as a vulnerable man into all the particular fragility of our human loves and friendships. I love the way Jesus responds to Mary's beautiful, useless gesture and recognizes it as something that is always worthwhile, something that will live for ever, for all the carping and criticism of Judas, then and now.

This sonnet is the fruit of an 'Ignatian' meditation and shares with that tradition a 'composition of place' and an invitation to enter into and become part of a Gospel scene. Ignatius invites us in meditation not just to read the words of the story and let its images flicker before us as though we were distant spectators, but rather to engage our imaginations fully and come close: to be there, to engage our senses in every particular. We are to ask ourselves, what do I see? What do I hear? What scent fills the air? What might I touch or taste? And then to go further and let our very selves engage with the action. Whom do I meet? What might I say? How do I feel? So my sonnet opens with the lines:

> Come close with Mary, Martha, Lazarus,
> So close the candles flare with their soft breath.

My hope in this poem is to bring us, through the rich feast of the senses, through the mysterious intimacy of encounter, to a centre, a stillness, a sense of poise and balance, in which we can see fully and unflinchingly the suffering that Jesus embraces with us. But we may also see beyond it, and glimpse a little of the joy of restored relationship and renewed love that his outpouring of himself on the cross will bring.

For me there is something poignant and infinitely suggestive about the breaking open of the alabaster jar of precious ointment. The breaking itself is important because it is irrevocable, and so is the idea that in one sense it is, as Judas crudely observes, a 'wasteful' or useless gesture, while at the same time being, as Jesus counters, 'a beautiful thing'. My understanding of this passage was deepened and transformed by conversation with one of my parishioners, now in heaven. She had a daughter who was multiply disabled. Brain damaged and confined to a wheelchair, she could hardly recognize, respond to or communicate with those around her, but her mother poured out years of love and care for her before the girl eventually died. And she told me once how, when she was despairing, heartbroken and ready to give up, the image suddenly came to her of Mary and the broken jar of ointment. She realized that this, in her own way, was who she was and what she was doing: pouring out every day the unreturnable love and care that so many in society might think, like Judas, was a 'waste', but was somehow, in spite of everything, renewing a beauty and a hope.

MAUNDY THURSDAY

Maundy Thursday *Malcolm Guite*

Here is the source of every sacrament,
The all-transforming presence of the Lord,
Replenishing our every element,
Remaking us in his creative Word.
For here the earth herself gives bread and wine,
The air delights to bear his Spirit's speech,
The fire dances where the candles shine,
The waters cleanse us with his gentle touch.
And here he shows the full extent of love
To us whose love is always incomplete,
In vain we search the heavens high above,
The God of love is kneeling at our feet.
Though we betray him, though it is the night.
He meets us here and loves us into light.

There is so much happening on this day, so many threads of connection flowing to and from this deep source of love and gospel vision. My sonnet for this central and sacramental day can only suggest one or two of them. We spent time in Passiontide reflecting, through several poems, on the garden of Gethsemane, so in this poem I want to take us back to a little earlier in the day, to those all-transforming events in the upper room. The meditation I present in this sonnet is centred, like the C. S. Lewis poem we looked at earlier, on the ancient idea of the four elements of earth, air, water and fire. Everything, ourselves included, was held to be a subtle combination of these four essential elements of creation, and it struck me as I contemplated the events of Maundy Thursday, with the foot-washing and the first communion, that all these elements of the old creation are taken up by Jesus and transformed in the making of the new. Jesus is both the fully human companion, cleansing his friends with a gentle touch, sharing his last supper with them, showing the fullness of his love, and also the Word, God in his full creative and shaping power, the One in and through whom everyone in that room and every element of the world is sustained in the beauty and particularity of its being. What we witness in the birth of the sacraments is both a human drama and a divine act of new creation. A sacrament is 'an outward and visible sign of an inward and spiritual grace' and it is certainly true that every word and gesture here, and each of the four elements, becomes a sign of God's redemptive love reaching us in Christ, from the cleansing water to the breaking and sharing of the bread and wine.

It is the Word himself who says of that bread, 'This is my Body': the same Word through whose utterance everything that is becomes itself. When this Word speaks, then something substantial, and new, is brought into existence. From his words in that room, to his Word dwelling richly in our hearts, the *novum mandatum*, the new commandment from which this day takes its name, springs into being. So too does the new reality of our communion with him physically in his body and his blood. There is on this day, therefore, a renewal of incarnation, an opening out of its fuller meaning. The body and blood he took for our sakes, woven in Mary's womb, is shared with us as he shares our nature, extended to and through us, so that we too are Christ's Body. Amazingly and wonderfully, he who took our human nature shares with us his divine nature. The Spirit is here for us to breathe, the substance of the true God is there with us, not high and inaccessible as Isaiah found it when he saw the Lord mighty and lifted up, but close, humbled below us, kneeling at our feet to wash us, or broken and placed into our hands to feed us.

And all this happens 'on the night that he was betrayed'. It is not when we have already purged ourselves and attained some long-sought moral height that these things are offered to us. It is here and now, in the confusion and ambiguity of our daily life, in the midst of our darkness and disloyalty, here where we need him most, where he meets us:

Though we betray him, though it is the night.
He meets us here and loves us into light.

GOOD FRIDAY

XII Jesus dies on the cross *Malcolm Guite*

The dark nails pierce him and the sky turns black
We watch him as he labours to draw breath.
He takes our breath away to give it back,
Return it to its birth through his slow death.
We hear him struggle, breathing through the pain,
Who once breathed out his spirit on the deep,
Who formed us when he mixed the dust with rain
And drew us into consciousness from sleep.
His Spirit and his life he breathes in all,
Mantles his world in his one atmosphere,
And now he comes to breathe beneath the pall
Of our pollutions, draw our injured air
To cleanse it and renew. His final breath
Breathes and bears us through the gates of death.

There is both so much and so little to be said on Good Friday. In some ways the Gospels, with their terse, spare narrative, give us the blank fact that brings us to a standstill: 'And they crucified him.' We can just stay with that and look, seeing things as they are. Or we can draw breath and try, year after year, to articulate what this means, and has gone on meaning for us.

In this sonnet, one of the 15 I wrote for the Stations of the Cross, meditating on Christ's final breath, I return to and draw on the words we encountered earlier in our pilgrimage, in George Herbert's poem 'Prayer': 'God's breath in man returning to his birth'.

Herbert's poem invites us into a very early tradition of prayer and meditation rooted in a reflection on the image of breath and breathing in the Bible. The two biblical languages, Hebrew and Greek, use a single word to mean both 'breath' and 'spirit'. 'God's breath in man' evokes that primal image in Genesis of God breathing the breath of life into humanity, the moment of our wakening as living beings, a moment of tender closeness to our Maker. But after that *inspiration* comes the equally decisive moment of *expiration*. We have to trace our history through fall and alienation, pain, sin and death, at last to the foot of the cross where a second Adam, one in whom also the whole of humanity is bound and involved, stretches out his arms to embrace the pain of the world and breathes back to God that gift of life: 'Then Jesus, crying with a loud voice, said "Father, into your hands I commend my spirit." Having said this, he breathed his last' (Luke 23.46).

Then we must look beyond the cross, to the resurrection and the new breath of life that comes with the sending of the Holy Spirit. John's account consciously parallels the first gift of the breath of life in Genesis: 'When he had said this, he breathed on them and said to them, "Receive the Holy Spirit"' (John 20.22).

Contained in the pattern of our breathing is the whole story of our salvation. For a Christian in prayer the very act of breathing can become a return to our birth: a receiving of original life from the breath of God, as we breathe in with Adam in the garden of our beginnings; an offering of all that needs letting go and redeeming as we breathe out with Christ on the cross; a glad acceptance of new life in the Holy Spirit as we breathe in again receiving our life and commission afresh from the risen Lord.

At the end of the sonnet I return to the image I had hinted at in the cleansing of the temple, that as Jesus breathed his last the veil in the temple was torn in two from top to bottom. A barrier has been broken, a gate has been opened. We are through at last.

HOLY SATURDAY

XIII Jesus' body is taken down from the cross
Malcolm Guite

His spirit and his life he breathes in all,
Now on this cross his body breathes no more.
Here at the centre everything is still,
Spent, and emptied, opened to the core.
A quiet taking down, a prising loose,
A cross-beam lowered like a weighing scale,
Unmaking of each thing that had its use,
A long withdrawing of each bloodied nail.
This is ground zero, emptiness and space
With nothing left to say or think or do,
But look unflinching on the sacred face
That cannot move or change or look at you.
Yet in that prising loose and letting be
He has unfastened you and set you free.

XIV Jesus is laid in the tomb *Malcolm Guite*

Here at the centre everything is still,
Before the stir and movement of our grief
Which bears its pain with rhythm, ritual,
Beautiful useless gestures of relief.
So they anoint the skin that cannot feel
And soothe his ruined flesh with tender care,
Kissing the wounds they know they cannot heal,

With incense scenting only empty air.
He blesses every love that weeps and grieves,
And makes our grief the pangs of a new birth.
The love that's poured in silence at old graves
Renewing flowers, tending the bare earth,
Is never lost. In him all love is found
And sown with him, a seed in the rich ground.

Holy Saturday is a strange, still day, hanging in an unresolved poise between the darkness of the day before and the light that is not yet with us. It has its own patterns and rituals that take up a little of that empty space of waiting. Children come into church to make an Easter Garden, exhausted clergy give themselves the space to venture a walk with their families and draw breath before tomorrow's big declamations. Those who have passed through the intense experience of a three-hour Good Friday watch service feel strangely dislocated from the crowds of Easter Bank Holiday shoppers that surge around the Saturday markets, and all the while for the faithful who have made this journey through Holy Week together there is a kind of emptiness and expectant stillness within.

I have tried to reflect a little of this in these two sonnets, which follow in sequence from yesterday's poem. I was conscious as I wrote them of how these great Christian festivals, especially Easter and Christmas, draw up and carry with them some of our deepest family memories. If we are going to remember and miss someone we have loved and lost, we will do it now. So in the second sonnet I move from a contemplation of the women bearing spices, wishing they could at least anoint the one they miss, to focus on the many people who will visit graves and memorial plaques over this weekend, 'renewing flowers, tending the bare earth'. All those 'beautiful useless gestures', all that 'love poured out in silence' are, I believe, somehow gathered together in these three days and sown deep in the ground of God's love, ready for the day when he will make all things new again.

EASTER SUNDAY

Easter *George Herbert*

Rise heart; thy Lord is risen. Sing his praise
Without delays,
Who takes thee by the hand, that thou likewise
With him mayst rise.
That, as his death calcined thee to dust,
His life may make thee gold, and much more just.

Awake, my lute, and struggle for thy part
With all thy art.
The cross taught all wood to resound his name,
Who bore the same.
His stretched sinews taught all strings, what key
Is best to celebrate this most high day.

Consort both heart and lute, and twist a song
Pleasant and long:
Or since all music is but three parts vied
And multiplied;
O let thy blessed Spirit bear a part,
And make up our defects with his sweet art.

I got me flowers to straw thy way:
I got me boughs off many a tree:
But thou wast up by break of day,
And brought'st thy sweets along with thee.

The Sun arising in the East,
Though he give light, and th'East perfume;
If they should offer to contest
With thy arising, they presume.

Can there be any day but this,
Though many suns to shine endeavour?
We count three hundred, but we miss:
There is but one, and that one ever.

For the last poem in this journey together, on this day of glorious beginnings, we return to George Herbert who has been such a companion and guide to us throughout.

So much of George Herbert's poetry is in a kind of hidden dialogue, a call and response with the Book of Common Prayer and the Bible that he knew so well. So in this poem his starting point is Psalm 57.8–11, one of the proper psalms for Easter Day Matins, and especially verse 8: 'Awake up, my glory, awake, lute and harp: I myself will awake right early' (BCP).

Herbert responds to this psalmic injunction with the words, 'Rise heart; thy Lord is risen', and in the second verse, 'Awake, my lute'. He has sung the psalm in his 'common prayer', his public worship, and now he is applying it within himself and to his whole day. But as so often in that application the personal becomes the present, the tactile, the deft, the courteous. The risen Christ of Easter is not, in this first verse, the cosmic Pantocrator but the familiar friend or lover who offers you a hand as you rise in the morning:

Who takes thee by the hand, that thou likewise
With him mayst rise.

And then, in one of Herbert's sudden luminous shifts, the poem takes an alchemical turn:

That, as his death calcined thee to dust,
His life may make thee gold, and much more just.

'Calcined' was the term used by alchemists for the fierce heat that burns away impurity, bringing whatever passes through the flame to a purer state. So another poet of the time could write, 'Yet you by a chaste Chimicke Art/Calcine frail love to pietie' (William Habington, in Wilcox, p. 141). And after that 'calcining' experience of Good Friday, Easter brings the great transmutation of which Herbert had spoken in his other alchemical poem, 'The Elixir': 'this is the famous stone that turneth all to gold'. But the transformative element is not a fabled 'philosopher's stone', it is new life in Jesus Christ: 'His life may make thee gold'.

So in the first verse Herbert calls on his heart to rise. He echoes the psalm of Matins, even as he is preparing himself for the Eucharist with its 'Sursum corda': 'lift up your hearts'. In the second verse, again following the morning psalm, he calls upon his lute:

> Awake, my lute, and struggle for thy part
> With all thy art.

And here he leaves alchemy behind and begins some beautifully extended musical metaphors. First he presents the daring and beautiful idea that

> The cross taught all wood to resound his name,
> Who bore the same.

Terse lines evoke a kind of mystical empathy in which even the wood of his own lute is somehow blessed and transformed in the blessing of all wood when the maker of the world was stretched on the tree. And that stretching itself leads to another, and even more daring metaphor:

> His stretched sinews taught all strings, what key
> Is best to celebrate this most high day.

The stretched strings of lute and viol were, of course, in Herbert's day literally visceral: organic lines of gut which, stretched and struck, set up a sympathetic resonance in the wood. Indeed this whole poem is a kind of theology of resonance; of our tuned response to the striking music of Christ's sacrifice. Herbert's own language here is extraordinarily sensitive and resonant, so the phrase 'The cross taught all wood to resound his name' carries in the word 'taught' also the sense of the tautness of the strings evoked in the next few lines. Even on Easter Day Herbert looks back to Good Friday and in the light of Easter sees Christ's 'stretched sinew' on the cross making a new music.

So Herbert's heart and lute are brought together in a 'consort', a word that meant both a musical ensemble and a social harmony. But is it enough? No, in the third verse Herbert brings in, draws in, the Spirit, the breath that Jesus exhaled to bring us new life. He does so through another fine musical metaphor. The basis of all harmony is the triad – all music is 'but three parts vied and multiplied' – so Herbert needs a third part, to join lute and heart, and he invokes the Spirit:

> O let thy blessed Spirit bear a part,
> And make up our defects with his sweet art.

The heart is our inner feeling, the lute is the art and skill with which those inner feelings find outward expression, but neither is complete without the Spirit that gives life to all, that prays within us when we do not know how to pray. And here the Spirit comes not as an overwhelming or overmastering experience from above, but alongside us, as a fellow musician who has come with us to 'bear a part'.

So at the end of the first part of the poem Herbert is awake, his lute is tuned, he has found in the spirit an accompanist and he is ready to begin the song. It is the song itself that forms the second part of the poem.

This lovely lyric adapts the courtly tradition of the 'aubade', the lovers' poem at dawn, and here Herbert playfully suggests that even the 'Sun arising in the East' would be presumptuous to compete or contend with the rising of this true Son. Indeed, the final verse claims that Easter Day is the only day: 'Can there be any day but this ...? We count three hundred but we miss', he says, meaning the 365 (rounded to 300) days of the year are wrongly counted – 'we miss'! There is only ever one day, the true Easter.

We have been travelling together in this book through 48 days together, but if George Herbert is right, it has only been one day! From now on there is just the single, eternal day of resurrection, and by its light we can look back over our long pilgrimage and see the glory of this day, hidden once but shining now, in all we have been through.

APPENDIX

Springs and Oases:
The Saints' Days in Lent

27 FEBRUARY:
GEORGE HERBERT (1593–1633)

George Herbert *Malcolm Guite*

Gentle exemplar, help us in our trials
With all that passed between you and your Lord,
That intimate exchange of frowns and smiles
Which chronicled your love-match with the Word.
Your manuscript, entrusted to a friend,
Has been entrusted now to every soul,
We make a new beginning in your end
And find your broken heart has made us whole.
Time has transplanted you, and you take root,
Past changing in the paradise of Love.
Help me to trace your Temple, tune your lute,
And listen for an echo from above.
Open the window, let me hear you sing,
And see the Word with you in everything.

Today the Church keeps the memory of George Herbert, who
has been so strong a companion with us on our Lenten journey.
Shortly before he died he sent the precious manuscript of his
poems to his friend Nicholas Ferrar at Little Gidding, asking
him to publish them only if he thought that they might 'turn to
the advantage of any dejected poor soul', but otherwise to burn
them. Fortunately for us Ferrar realized what a treasure he had
been given and took them to Cambridge to be published as *The*

Temple. They have been in print ever since, and have turned to the spiritual advantage of countless souls.

This sonnet reflects on a number of Herbert's poems, but particularly on his masterpiece 'The Flower'. In that poem he imagines himself as a flower, sometimes blossoming, sometimes shrivelled back to its mother-root, but somehow still capable of recovery:

> Who would have thought my shrivel'd heart
> Could have recover'd greennesse? It was gone
>   Quite under ground; as flowers depart
> To see their mother-root, when they have blown;
>   Where they together
>   All the hard weather,
> Dead to the world, keep house unknown.

But, as he goes through these traumas of loss and recovery, an inevitable part of our being in time, he longs, in a beautiful metaphor, to be transplanted at last into the true paradise of heaven:

> O that I once past changing were;
> Fast in thy Paradise, where no flower can wither!

So my sonnet celebrates the fact that he is now where he longed to be, in the place he had glimpsed 'through the glass' in 'The Elixir'. 'The Flower' also contains the beautiful and mysterious lines:

> We say amisse,
>   This or that is:
>   Thy word is all, if we could spell.

Just as 'Easter' suggests that there is really only one true day, shining through the 'three hundred', so here, in a moment of mystical intuition, Herbert senses that the one Word shines through and undergirds the myriad things we encounter, and I allude to this at the conclusion of my sonnet.

1 MARCH: ST DAVID

Miracle on St David's Day *Gillian Clarke*

They flash upon that inward eye
Which is the bliss of solitude.
The Daffodils, William Wordsworth

An afternoon yellow and open-mouthed
with daffodils. The sun treads the path
among cedars and enormous oaks.
It might be a country house, guests strolling,
the rumps of gardeners between nursery shrubs.

I am reading poetry to the insane.
An old woman, interrupting, offers
as many buckets of coals as I need.
A beautiful chestnut-haired boy listens
entirely absorbed. A schizophrenic

on a good day, they tell me later.
In a cage of first March sun a woman
sits not listening, not seeing, not feeling.
In her neat clothes the woman is absent.
A big mild man is tenderly led

to his chair. He has never spoken.
His labourer's hands on his knees,
he rocks gently to the rhythms of the poems.
I read to their presences, absences,
to the big, dumb labouring man as he rocks.

He is suddenly standing, silently,
huge and mild, but I feel afraid. Like slow
movement of spring water or the first bird
of the year in the breaking darkness,
the labourer's voice recites 'The Daffodils'.

The nurses are frozen, alert; the patients
seem to listen. He is hoarse but word-perfect.
Outside the daffodils are still as wax,
a thousand, ten thousand, their syllables
unspoken, their creams and yellows still.

Forty years ago, in a Valleys school,
the class recited poetry by rote.
Since the dumbness of misery fell
he has remembered there was a music
of speech and that once he had something to say.

When he's done, before the applause, we observe
the flowers' silence. A thrush sings
and the daffodils are aflame.

Today the Church celebrates St David's Day, which is also kept
as a national day in Wales. He probably flourished in the sixth
century, or possibly earlier, and while many sites and foundations
have associations with him, it is difficult to know much for certain
about the incidents of his life. His reputed last words, however,
supposedly given in a sermon on the day before he died, have an
authentic ring and have proved popular: 'Be joyful, and keep your
faith and your creed, and do the little things that you have seen
me do and heard about. I will walk the path that our fathers have
trod before us.'

For the National Saint of Wales I have chosen a poem by the
National Poet of Wales, Gillian Clarke. This beautiful poem,
'Miracle on St David's Day', tells the true story of how she was
giving a poetry reading in a mental hospital on St David's Day.
Both the ward and the gardens outside were full of daffodils, and

suddenly a man who had been silent his whole time in the hospital stood up and recited Wordsworth's 'Daffodils' poem from memory. Asked in an interview what she thought had made him recite the poem, Gillian Clarke replied:

> I think two things set the poem going in his mind. One was the daffodils in the room and in the grass outside. The other was that I was reading poetry. The rhythm of the poems and the sight of the daffodils reminded him that he had loved poetry once, and the moment set him free from dumbness.

That sense of the rhythm and music of poetry unlocking and releasing something inside us seems an essential insight, and one of the reasons why it is good to fold poetry into our prayer life. What she says of this man, suddenly released into speech, might hold true for many of us:

> Since the dumbness of misery fell
> he has remembered there was a music
> of speech and that once he had something to say.

The early Celtic saints, among whom David is numbered, had a reputation for a kind of 'nature mysticism', for responding to the beauty of the world around them and sensing, sometimes, the presence of the divine flaming through it. It seems appropriate, therefore, that this poem with St David in its title should end on one of those moments of transfiguration:

> we observe
> the flowers' silence. A thrush sings
> and the daffodils are aflame.

17 MARCH: ST PATRICK

St Patrick *Malcolm Guite*

Six years a slave, and then you slipped the yoke,
Till Christ recalled you, through your captors' cries!
Patrick, you had the courage to turn back,
With open love to your old enemies,
Serving them now in Christ, not in their chains,
Bringing the freedom He gave you to share.
You heard the voice of Ireland, in your veins
Her passion and compassion burned like fire.

Now you rejoice amidst the three-in-one,
Refreshed in love and blessing all you knew,
Look back on us and bless us, Ireland's son,
And plant the staff of prayer in all we do:
A gospel seed that flowers in belief,
A greening glory, coming into leaf.

While Patrick is, of course, primarily associated with Ireland where he flourished as a missionary in the second half of the fifth century, he was not Irish to begin with. He seems to have been a shepherd on the mainland of Great Britain and was captured there, at the age of 16, by raiding pirates and taken across the sea to Ireland where he was sold as a slave. He was six years in captivity before he finally made his escape and returned to Britain. And this is where the story takes a truly extraordinary turn. While he was enslaved in Ireland, working as a shepherd for his masters, Patrick became a Christian. When, having made good his escape,

he returned home, he had a vision in which a man gave him a let-
ter headed 'The Voice of Ireland'. It urged him to go back to the
very place from which he had escaped and bring the gospel to his
former captors! That Patrick obeyed such a vision seems to me a
greater miracle than any of the others subsequently attributed to
him, and it is on this return that my sonnet turns. That capacity
to return, face and forgive former oppressors or enemies seems a
particularly vital gift for Ireland's patron to bestow. As well as
alluding briefly to 'St Patrick's Breastplate', my sonnet touches
on the story that wherever Patrick planted his staff to pray, it
blossomed.

20 MARCH: ST CUTHBERT

Cuddy *Malcolm Guite*

Cuthbertus says the dark stone up in Durham
Where I have come on pilgrimage to pray.
But not this great cathedral, nor the solemn
Weight of Norman masonry we lay
Upon your bones could hold your soul in prison.
Free as the Cuddy ducks they named for you,
Loosed by the lord who died to pay your ransom,
You roam the North just as you used to do;
Always on foot and walking with the poor,
Breaking the bread of angels in your cave,
A sanctuary, a sign, an open door,
You follow Christ through keening wind and wave,
To be and bear with him where all is borne;
The heart of heaven, in your Inner Farne.

Today is St Cuthbert's Day. Cuthbert, or 'Cuddy' as the locals still call him, is one of those in the 'cloud of witness' I am particularly glad to have as a companion on my journey. He had a vision on the night that Aidan, the saintly founder of the monastery at Lindisfarne, died, and that was the moment that a vocation that would weave him closely into the story of Holy Island began. He became in his turn Aidan's successor as Bishop of Lindisfarne, but understood his role not as an ecclesiastical administrator but as an itinerant preacher and teacher. Offered a horse by the king to help him on his travels, he gave it to the first beggar he met. He continued on foot, sharing his journeys and breaking bread with the poor of Northumberland. His shrine in Durham Cathedral is always a place of pilgrimage for me, but as I emphasize in this sonnet, his free spirit is not to be held back by the great weight of Norman masonry, or the conventional piety that later generations have laid on him.

25 MARCH:
THE ANNUNCIATION

The Annunciation *Edwin Muir*

The angel and the girl are met.
Earth was the only meeting place.
For the embodied never yet
Travelled beyond the shore of space.
The eternal spirits in freedom go.

See, they have come together, see,
While the destroying minutes flow,
Each reflects the other's face
Till heaven in hers and earth in his
Shine steady there. He's come to her
From far beyond the farthest star,
Feathered through time. Immediacy

Of strangest strangeness is the bliss
That from their limbs all movement takes.
Yet the increasing rapture brings
So great a wonder that it makes
Each feather tremble on his wings.

Outside the window footsteps fall
Into the ordinary day
And with the sun along the wall
Pursue their unreturning way.
Sound's perpetual roundabout
Rolls its numbered octaves out
And hoarsely grinds its battered tune.

But through the endless afternoon
These neither speak nor movement make,
But stare into their deepening trance
As if their gaze would never break

It seems appropriate that one of the little 'interludes' in Lent, the little lifts from penitence into praise, should be the feast of the Annunciation. This feast falls nine months before Christmas, and always within Lent. But if Lent is in part about turning our attention back to God, about coming close to him and preparing ourselves to respond with joyful and obedient hearts to his presence in our lives, then this feast gives us the very epitome of openness, discernment and response! This is the day we remember how the angel Gabriel came to the Virgin Mary with the bliss and the blessing of heaven, with the promise of the coming Holy Spirit and the glory of the Saviour to be born. It is the story of how, in Mary's courageous and open 'Yes' to God, Jesus – God's own 'Yes' to all humanity – was conceived and came into the world. With this glimpse in the midst of Lent we look forward to Christmas, and to the gift with which our own true life begins. Edwin Muir's great poem seems to go to the heart of the mystery. As with 'The Incarnate One', which we read on Passion Sunday, Muir has a very strong sense of the rootedness and particularity of this world as the only place where our faith can become substantiated and real. He says in this poem, 'Earth was the only meeting place', and though he says that we, the embodied, 'never yet travelled beyond the shore of space' he nevertheless shows how in the Annunciation that the eternal can come to us where we are. In that meeting there is awe and mystery on both sides!

For the angel too there is an 'immediacy of strangest strangeness' which is his bliss.

The poem leaves us with a beautiful account not just of the Annunciation but also of moments we ourselves may have experienced in which, although other things may be going on around us, sounds and events falling into 'the ordinary day', we ourselves seem to have been lifted out of time into an eternal and beautiful stasis.

References

Browning, Elizabeth Barrett, *Aurora Leigh*, Oxford World Classics, Oxford University Press, 2008.

Chesterton, G. K., 'The Hammer of God', in *The Innocence of Father Brown*, collected in *The Father Brown Stories*, Folio Press, 1996.

Clarke, Gillian, interview on Sheer Poetry website (www.sheer-poetry.co.uk/gcse/gillian-clarke/notes-on-gillian-clarke-poems/miracle-on-st-david-s-day).

Coleridge, Samuel Taylor, *Biographia Literaria*, Vol. II, edited by James Engell and W. Jackson Bate, Princeton, 1983.

Guite, Malcolm, *Faith, Hope and Poetry*, Ashgate, 2010.

Guite, Malcolm, *Sounding the Seasons*, Canterbury Press, 2012.

Heaney, Seamus, *Opened Ground*, Faber and Faber, 2002.

Heaney, Seamus, *The Redress of Poetry*, Faber and Faber, 1995.

Isba, Anne, *Gladstone*, Boydell & Brewer, 2006.

LeClercq, Jean, *The Love of Learning and the Desire for God*, SPCK, 1978.

Lefebure, Molly, *Samuel Taylor Coleridge: A Bondage of Opium*, Quartet Books, 1977.

Lewis, C. S., 'Is Theology Poetry', lecture to the Oxford Socratic Club, 1945, in *The Weight of Glory and Other Addresses*, Macmillan, 1980.

Lewis, C. S., *The Great Divorce*, Geoffrey Bles, 1945.

Lewis, C. S., 'The Inner Ring', Memorial Lecture at King's College, University of London, 1944.

Lewis, C. S., *The Lion the Witch and the Wardrobe*, Harper Collins Children's Books, 2011.

Wilcox, Helen (ed.), *The English Poems of George Herbert*, Cambridge University Press, 2010.

Acknowledgements

I 'road-tested' most of these poems with a Lent Group at the church of St Edward King and Martyr in Cambridge. I am grateful to them for their comments and feedback which have helped me in framing some of the short prose commentaries to the poetry in this volume.

Kelly Belmonte, 'How I talk to God', in *Three Ways of Searching*, Finishing Line Press, 2013. Reprinted by kind permission of the author.

Gillian Clarke, 'A Miracle on St David's Day', in *Gillian Clarke: Collected Poems*, Carcanet, 1997. Reprinted by kind permission of the publishers.

Dante: the passages from Dante are taken from *The Divine Comedy, I Inferno* and *II Purgatorio*, translated by Robin Kirkpatrick, Penguin Classics, 2006 and 2007. Reprinted by kind permission of the translator.

Malcolm Guite: the selection of my poems is drawn from my two volumes with Canterbury Press, *Sounding the Seasons* (2012) and *The Singing Bowl* (2013). Reprinted by kind permission of the publisher. 'St Patrick' appears in print here for the first time. Some of my commentary on the poems of Davies, Herbert and Heaney is drawn from work I did for *Faith, Hope and Poetry*, Ashgate, 2010.

Seamus Heaney, 'Station Island XI' and 'Postscript', in *Opened*

Ground: Poems 1966–1996, Faber and Faber, 1998. Reprinted by permission of the publishers.

John Heath-Stubbs, 'Golgotha', in *John Heath-Stubbs Selected Poems*, Carcanet, 1990. Reprinted by permission of the publisher.

C. S. Lewis, 'Love is as warm as tears', in *Collected Poems*, Fount, 1994. Reprinted by permission of the Lewis Estate.

Gwyneth Lewis, 'Homecoming', in *Parables and Faxes*, Bloodaxe, 1995. Reprinted by kind permission of the author.

Czeslaw Milosz, 'Late Ripeness', in *New and Collected Poems 1931–2001*, Penguin Modern Classics Poetry, 2006. Reprinted by permission of the publisher.

Edwin Muir, 'The Incarnate One' and 'The Annunciation', in *Collected Poems 1921–1958*, Faber and Faber, 1960. Reprinted by permission of the publisher.

Holly Ordway, 'Maps', in *Dappled Things: A Quarterly of Ideas, Art, and Faith*, Spring 2013. Reprinted by kind permission of the publisher.

R. S. Thomas, 'The Bright Field', in *Laboratories of the Spirit*, Macmillan, 1975. Reprinted with permission from the R. S. Thomas Estate.

Rowan Williams, 'Gethsemane', in *The Poems of Rowan Williams*, Perpetua Press, 2002. Reprinted by permission of the author.